One Year Sober

How I Quit Drinking and You Can Too

Bill Williams

DEDICATION

This book is dedicated to all the brave warriors who benefit from reading it.

CONTENTS

Acknowledgments

1	I Suck at Drinking	1
2	Who Is This Book For?	4
3	Do I Have a Problem?	6
4	My Story	9
5	Why Alcohol Sucks	15
6	Moderation	23
7	What is an Alcoholic?	27
8	The Grief of Giving up Alcohol	31
9	How to Beat Cravings	36
10	Have a Plan	40
11	A Recovery Mindset	44
12	What to Expect at an Alcoholics Anonymous Meeting	51
13	Recovering Alcoholics are Fun!	56
14	Relapse - Have a Lifeline	60
15	My Higher Power Story	62
16	Are We Crazy?	65

17	The Insanity of Alcohol	67
18	Why I Drank	69
19	Christmas In A Bottle	73
20	I Cry at Meetings	75
21	Stop Digging	77
22	What Kind of Alcoholic are You?	79
23	YMBAAI - You Might be an Alcoholic If	81
24	Music Can Set You Free	87
25	At One Year	93
26	Resources	104

ACKNOWLEDGMENTS

I would like to thank the many people who have helped me to get sober and also those who encouraged me to write this book.

First off, I would like to thank my wife. She is an incredible, strong willed woman who has stuck with me through thick and thin. At the worst of my drinking, I was not a good partner by any stretch of the imagination. I have no idea why she stood by me for all those years, but I am so grateful that she did. We are so much happier now that I am sober.

I would also like to thank Alcoholics Anonymous. Without them, I would still be drinking today. AA is such an incredible organization — self-supporting and utterly humble, run by the fellowship itself and helping so many all over the world. It is truly an amazing organization giving people the opportunity to rebuild their lives with others like themselves. So many people in the rooms have helped me through sharing their stories. I learned something from each of them. They remind me where I was, where I am, and where I want to go.

My sponsor Jack got me started on the steps. He is a shining example of what AA is all about. Twenty years younger than myself with nine years sober, he took me under his wing and guided me through the steps. I will forever be in his debt for being so selfless with his service and in giving up his time to help save me. We had so many conversations and became such good friends through my recovery that he probably knows me better than anyone. I am so thankful for the deep friendships that I have formed on this journey — some of the most meaningful ones in my life.

I would also like to thank Cafe:RE and all the great friends that I made online there (see the Resources chapter for more information). It's a wonderfully convenient way to get support and to also be of service to others taking this journey. I don't know what I would have done without Cafe Jim's enlightening videos, Tom's witted humor, Christie's "you need to hear it" tough love, Sara's thoughtful comments, or Kris's amazing insights and support as a bedrock member of the group. Many of you reviewed this book and I thank you for your thoughts and suggestions. There are so many others to mention, all incredible people giving alcohol the boot!

I want to thank Paul Churchill for his incredible *Recovery Elevator* podcast, his Cafe:RE support group, and his amazing attitude. Long before I ever went to AA, I was listening to Paul's podcast. Hours and hours of Paul's insights and thoughts as well as his guest's stories chipped away at my ability to continue to ignore my drinking problem. I never would have gotten sober without your podcast deprogramming my mind, Paul. Thanks for ruining alcohol for me, brother — I love you!

Finally, I want to thank you all for buying and reading this book. We have an addiction epidemic in this country and I am convinced that the only way to fix it is through education, understanding, acceptance, and action. Our stories put a personal face on addiction and we realize that the addict is not just some nameless stranger, but also our neighbors and loved ones.

Please feel free to contact me at tom.phoenix@gmail.com. I love hearing from people who have read my essays. If you liked the book, please take a minute to rate and review it on Amazon. Your rating will help others to find it, read these essays, and start their journey to become sober.

1 I SUCK AT DRINKING

I suck at drinking. It took me many years to figure that out, but it is absolutely true. I started drinking at fourteen and drank normally for the next fifteen years. At that time, I thought I had drinking all figured out. I was a pro! In college, I really had it down. I could party two, three, or four nights a week and still maintain straight A's, no problem. I eased off a bit once I graduated, but I maintained friendships where I would often drink, occasionally binge on the weekends, and regularly meet for cocktails. For the next twenty years, my career was skyrocketing and I was living the dream. I met a wonderful woman, got married, had kids, and started several businesses. I had it all figured out. Until, I didn't. I finally came to understand that, despite being a veteran expert at it, I truly sucked at drinking and needed to stop.

I wrote this book and these essays as part of my recovery. Writing them has helped me to both get and stay sober. When I gave up drinking alcohol, it was not easy. I used writing as a key tool to process and understand what I was feeling during my recovery. I wrote these essays for myself to clarify my thoughts and to better understand what was happening.

After a few months, I shared my essays with a friend because I thought they might help her. Her reaction was immediate and surprising. She was extremely grateful and suggested that I publish them to help others. I started a blog where I could share my thoughts with friends who were also recovering and the response was also positive. After continued feedback that I should publish my essays, I decided to do so, and the result is the book you have in your hands right now.

I drank continually for thirty-five years, heavily for the last twenty, and suffered for the last three years. Then I quit. My drinking history as described above might seem extreme, but I think if you take a cursory look at your own, you may find that you too have been drinking continually for perhaps far too long. I no longer desire alcohol in the least. These essays describe elements of that journey in the hopes of helping others to stop drinking as well. They are a deeply personal, open and honest description of how I quit drinking.

I want to say upfront that I am not a doctor and I have no credentials in the treatment of addiction. I am just a regular guy who likes to write and who went to the school of hard knocks in getting a journeyman's education on alcohol, addiction, and recovery. Take what you can from the ideas I discuss. This is what has worked for me, and I truly believe it can work for you as well. These stories are designed to present ideas and to encourage thinking and growth. As you read, concentrate on what works for you and save the rest for another day.

Finally, keep coming back and re-reading. As you progress through not drinking, you will need to hear different messages. What is of little interest to you now, could be of great help to you in a few months. I hope that you   enjoy   my   essays.

2 WHO IS THIS BOOK FOR?

Who did I write this book for? There are several readers that can greatly benefit from reading this book.

The primary reader is a drinker like me who has decided they may have an issue with alcohol in their life and want to do something about it. Perhaps you have explored enough that you already know you should slow down or stop drinking and are looking for inspiration, help, encouragement, and some tips.

Another reader is anyone who has questions about their use of alcohol. Am I drinking too much or for the wrong reasons. Should I quit? Should I drink less? Do I need help? Should I reach out to others for help? While I do not directly answer these questions for you, my essays will help you to clarify your thinking in answering them for yourself.

Finally, this book is for anyone who is curious about alcohol or the drinker's relationship with it. You don't have to be a heavy drinker, a moderate drinker, or a drinker at all. Perhaps you simply want to better understand alcohol or have a loved one you are concerned about. It is difficult for non-drinkers to fully understand the compulsion of an obsessed drinker, and this book will give you some insight into why alcohol is so important to them.

Whoever you are, I will do my best to keep you entertained as we explore the true nature of alcohol and recovery.

3 DO I HAVE A PROBLEM?

If you are reading this book, then yes in all likelihood you do. I know that is not what you want to hear. I was once in your shoes. I understand how this works, but there you have it. Anyone who does not have an issue with alcohol would not have read this far. If you really want to convince yourself, google "Do I have a drinking problem?" and take a test on one of the many links that come up.

Ask yourself this question: What is the value proposition of drinking alcohol? Make a list of both the positives and negatives of drinking and compare the two lists, much like you might do for any important decision in your life. What good comes to your life because of alcohol? Has anything negative ever happened to you or those you love that is related to alcohol? Stop, go now, write them down, and then come back.

Under positives, did you write relaxation from stress, anxiety reduction, relief from boredom, socialization, or fun? Many of us drink for these reasons, but the truth is that eventually alcohol actually makes us more depressed, more stressed, and less able to have fun. Think about what happens at the end of the evening of a night of drinking, the poor sleep, or the hangover and exhaustion the following day. If you can list negative experiences related to alcohol, you not only have an issue with alcohol, but you have just created a list of them.

It's important that you understand this is not your fault. We live in a culture that worships a highly addictive substance that most everyone is strongly encouraged to excessively drink on a regular basis. Anyone, absolutely all people, who drink alcohol in sufficient quantities and for a long enough period of time will become addicted to it. It's just how our brain works. For some it happens more quickly than others due to their genetic makeup much like how some of us are better singers, faster sprinters, or better at math. Given enough time and drinking, however, we all become heavy drinkers. It's a shame no one told us this truth about alcohol before we became obsessed with it, but we can't change the past. We must live in the now. The reality is that alcohol addiction is a huge sliding scale. While all drinkers will become progressively worse with time, everyone goes at their own individual pace. Some hit bottom in a few years and some may take decades. We all progress and also recover at our own pace and for our own reasons.

I began my journey to stop drinking based on a challenge. I had listened to a podcast that ran me through twelve questions to determine if I had a problem with alcohol. It was all very confusing to me, answering from one to five for each question and then summing those and comparing my total to a chart that indicated if I had a problem with alcohol. The entire time I was taking the test I was lying because, well, that's what we heavy drinkers do when asked about our drinking! After the test, the host acknowledged these complexities and said his litmus test is far easier. It's based on your reaction to a simple question. Are you ready? His question is this: How does the idea of giving up alcohol for thirty days make you feel? What is your immediate reaction? My answer was not only no, but hell no. I knew the longest I could do was a few days, maybe a week at best. I drank every day for over a decade, and not regularly drinking seemed like an alien concept to me. A person who is not dependent on alcohol would immediately answer "Thirty days, no problem at all." It would be no more difficult to give up than eating pickles for a month. I nervously decided to take up the challenge, and I have not had a drink since that day.

Despite what the alcohol marketers and lobbyists say, there is no safe or beneficial amount of alcohol for anyone to consume. Think about all the chaos and destruction that it has likely caused not only in your life, but in those that you have known. It's simply bad news. Consuming any amount of alcohol is a problem for your health. It is no more sane than deciding to drink lighter fluid.

Even if you are not yet ready to stop drinking because you feel that you do not have a problem, keep reading. Perhaps something will resonate with you. If you are going to keep drinking, you should at least know what lies ahead.

4 **MY STORY**

Let's get this out of the way. One thing I've found is that people obsessed with alcohol cannot understand the relationship that regular drinkers have with it. How can they stop after one drink? How can they open a bottle of wine on Monday, have two drinks during the week, and then dump the rest out at the end of the week? Why would someone want to drink and not get drunk? These ideas make no sense to the heavy drinker. The same goes in reverse. People who are not obsessed with alcohol don't understand why we don't simply stop or choose to drink less.

For these reasons, here is my story. I tell it so that you can understand my relationship with alcohol and how it has impacted my life. Once you read it, our relationship changes when you perhaps relate with some of my experience. By telling you my story, I am opening up and getting out of my comfort zone by being vulnerable and inviting you to share my journey. Sharing your story connects you to other people and you often become immediate friends. It's like you are suddenly dropped into the middle of a relationship that has been going on for years. I have professional friends I have known for years who I feel I barely know. At the same time, I have become strongly attached to others who have shared their alcohol struggles with me although we have only recently met. So, without further delay, this is my story….

My Story

I had my first drink at fourteen but was a regular drinker for many years. I call myself a functional alcoholic, mostly because I continually drank for the last thirty-five years while at the same time being very successful in my personal and professional life. I never had a DUI, lost a job, got in a fight, or wrecked my car because of alcohol.

We talk a lot about control and powerlessness in recovery. When I was drinking, I never felt out of control. In fact, controlling my alcohol consumption was a huge part of my life. I was all about control and thought of it constantly. I controlled everything in my life. However, I was powerless to fully stop drinking. I just couldn't stop and stay stopped. I would start drinking and then stop once I was drunk but could not stay stopped for more than a few days. I would drink most every night but not so much that I couldn't fulfill my life responsibilities the next morning by going to work and caring for my family. I wanted to quit most mornings but found myself once again drinking every night. It was all thoroughly progressive. Over the course of many years, I started first with a couple glasses and worked my way up to a couple bottles or more when I was free to recover the following day. As the years rolled on, it became increasingly difficult for me to recover sufficiently from my weekend drinking in order to report for work on Mondays. During my last year of drinking, I consistently called in sick or worked from home every Monday and often more than that.

I drank through the wind, snow, ice, rain, sickness, health, birthdays, funerals, at parties, by myself, and on all occasions all the time whenever I could. I would think about alcohol many times per day. I was obsessed with it. It was my God. Alcohol was my higher power.

I was shocked at the sheer amount I drank. Every alcoholic knows the recycle container drag of shame. There were so many empty bottles by the end of the week that it looked like I had thrown a block party. I spent hours each night, emptying them one at a time. In addition to hiding bottles in the house (the closet, the garage, my bathroom cabinet, behind the water heater, etc.), I've snuck them into the neighbors' recycling bin to look a little less screwed up. It was so embarrassing. I lied to everybody in my life about my drinking, including myself.

I don't have the crazy dramatic drinking stories I often hear in AA meetings. My story is more of slow, gradual, wasting of a life — as I got drunk to some degree most every night, but not too drunk, through my twenties, thirties, and forties. Sometimes I wish I had fallen harder or faster because I think it would have saved me decades of time. I drank in a mostly controlled but unstoppable manner for over twenty years. It took me ten to fifteen years to get started drinking, and then I had my groove on for the next twenty years or so with no real desire to quit. I drank with others but mostly drank alone. I loved alcohol. It helped me live my life and excel in my career. Alcohol and I accomplished great things together. I started several companies, held leadership and director roles, and created some great technology.

However, all that drinking started to finally catch up with me. I knew I had a problem and tried to quit many times during the last few years of my drinking. I tried many strategies to moderate, but nothing ever worked for me.

After a short time, I would be right back on the same merry-go-round. I remember watching the HBO *Westworld* television series and thinking that I was just like these robots. I was hopelessly looping through the same day again and again just going through the motions of a grand facade with no ability to hit the stop button and take a breath.

My bottom came when I pushed the amount that I was drinking due to some major new stresses in my life. The specifics of those stresses don't matter. What matters is that I coped with them how I now coped with anything that I didn't want to deal with in my life — I DRANK. Increasingly, I was no longer able to stop before becoming too drunk too often. My control was slipping away, and I was getting much less functional at life. Eventually, I became sick and tired of drinking and thinking about alcohol all the time. I knew life was more than this, and I also knew that I was killing myself with booze. I could no longer deny what alcohol was doing to me. I could feel my body was starting to fail. I knew that alcohol would eventually kill me.

I finally got serious about quitting. After doing it on my own for two weeks, which was about all I could manage in the past, I started going to AA. That made all the difference to me. Being in the company of others and having that common connection gave me strength, confidence, and hope. It's so inspiring to see people working through their struggles in transforming themselves and their lives. I attended meetings whenever I felt the urge to drink, which in the beginning, was often. I would hit at least three to four meetings per week, trying different ones in various parts of the city to find the group that felt like home to me. I threw myself into AA and began to connect with others. I went out of my way to stay in touch with people who had put alcohol in their rearview mirror. It wasn't long before I met someone I really connected with who was nine years sober. One night we were chatting, and he offered to take me through the steps — and just like that, I had a sponsor! I began to work the steps and to write about my experiences, and my life began to change for the better. I looked and felt healthier, more rested, and more at peace than I had in many years.

The first weeks and months weren't easy. I had frequent dreams about drinking, intense cravings, and a general restlessness. At two months of sobriety, I had an emergency surgery near-death experience that resulted in the complete removal of all desire for alcohol. I woke up from the surgery, and no longer craved alcohol. It was like they had cut it out of me. I still had much to do in working the steps with my sponsor and developing coping mechanisms to replace my old friend alcohol, but without the gnawing desire to drink, it was easier. My sobriety journey was well underway, and I kept at it. Now, I love being fully aware and intentionally living and fully experiencing my life. I am far more functional than ever without alcohol. I feel like I have the brain of a teenager — everything is so clear and vivid. I would not trade my sobriety for anything. I sometimes feel like Rip Van Winkle. I took a drink and slept for twenty years, and I am now fully awake and wondering how exactly this all happened.

In the end, getting drunk every night alone and still being able to perform at a highly successful level is not functional. It's a constant struggle for both your mind and body. I was cheating myself out of having an intentional life, my wife out of a better husband, my kids out of a better father, and my company out of a better employee. I'm grateful I quit drinking with the help of my new sober friends, and that I am now just plain-old all-around highly functional.

My advice to those I meet who question their use of alcohol is to face the problem right now and not waste another minute of their precious life. Be real, live with intention, and don't check out of your life. This obsession literally ends in the grave, and will absolutely kill you at some point. Life is so much better sober.

5 WHY ALCOHOL SUCKS

Paul Churchill of the *Recovery Elevator* podcast fame sums it up best when he regularly says on his podcast that "Alcohol is shit." No matter how you look at it, this simple conclusion is inescapable. Don't believe me? Let me run down my list of the crimes that alcohol is responsible for against humanity. Whenever I have a fleeting thought that I might drink again, I do two things. I first get myself to a fellowship meeting, and then I recommit to educating myself about what a truly horrific substance alcohol is.

How bad is alcohol? Let us count the ways. To start with, in no particular order, alcohol makes you fat, stupid, sick, tired and lazy. It frequently costs people their money, health, happiness, freedom, and even their lives.

Alcohol makes you fat for two reasons that few people understand. If you eat food and drink alcohol at the same time, and who doesn't, you will gain unwanted weight due to the way our bodies process food and alcohol. Your body has no ability to turn alcohol into fat, so it will immediately burn any alcohol you drink for energy. At the same time, it will turn any other food you have eaten directly into fat. What's more, we are much more likely to eat high fat food and more of it when we are drinking, so it's like a perfect storm. No wonder so many diets do not work. It's because the dieter is likely also drinking. Alcohol makes you fat. It's just basic biology. This is for ANY amount of alcohol, even small amounts. When I quit drinking, I lost so much weight that I couldn't believe it. I wasn't that overweight to begin with, but I lost a pound a week for six months with no effort on my part.

Alcohol makes you stupid. It prevents brain cells from communicating making us not only mentally slow but also dull. When we drink, it directly affects our motor skills, emotions, memory, ability to think, plan, solve problems, learn, or remember. That's basically the whole ball of wax! When we bathe our brain, the most incredible organ nature has ever produced, in alcohol, it ceases to function properly. Our brain, instead of being our most important tool for survival, becomes a complete liability to ourselves and others when it is exposed to alcohol. We become truly mentally impaired. Heavy drinkers who have been at it for many years suffer from more permanent cognitive decline such as dementia, Alzheimers, and a host of other brain issues including cancer. The latest studies show that even drinking light amounts of alcohol, the kind associated with social drinkers, damages the brain. I am a professional software developer which requires me to constantly learn and keep up with a vast amount of information on a daily basis. When I was hung over and working, I was far from reasonably functional. I was basically phoning it in at times. I am so grateful that I somehow did not develop permanent brain damage due to my drinking. I am better at my job today that I have been in decades and that feels amazing.

Alcohol makes you sick, tired, and lazy. First, alcohol is a depressant which literally will cause you to feel anxious, restless, and depressed. The reason you feel good when you initially drink it, but like hell later on and the next day, is that your brain, in an effort to fight off alcohol's depressing effect, will use the bodies chemicals to counteract the negative effects. It is literally making you high in order to avoid the alcohol induced upcoming low. No one would argue that a hangover doesn't make you feel sick. You are in no shape to seize the day. After a night of drinking, you are tired, probably have a headache, are sensitive to light and sounds, are dehydrated and thirsty, feel like vomiting, and are likely in one hell of a bad mood. You are truly sick, tired, and up for absolutely nothing. I know I was. It was truly terrible. I would wake up each morning feeling like hell, struggle through, and get to work where I felt sick until around noon when I was finally productive. By the time I got home around seven, I felt like drinking and would start the whole cycle all over again. I rode that merry-go-round for twenty years.

Alcohol makes you irritable, anxious, and stressed out. In the beginning, many first start drinking in order to relieve stress — a few drinks and it's like Calgon took me away! It's a cruel master however, because this effect is temporary. It works great for a long time, and then it stops working altogether and causes the very same symptoms it used to relieve. It's unbelievable, like some ironically sinister Greek mythology tale. In the beginning, alcohol acts as a depressive and analgesic to smooth out the stress. Later, once you have developed a tolerance and alcohol has modified your brain chemistry, your brain now needs it in order to reduce the stress. When the alcohol begins to leave your body, your stress, anxiety, and irritability levels start to climb with the result that you must drink more and more in order to maintain your sanity. I woke up each night at 3:30 like clockwork in a sweaty, heart-racing, fast breathing mess. I would get out of bed, drink a huge glass of water, towel off, put on a new shirt, and try to go back to sleep. Many nights it would take me hours of lying there in order to fall asleep for another hour or so before I had to wake up and start my day. It's a stressful way to live.

Alcohol makes you tired all the time because you cannot sleep soundly. When I was drinking, I stopped dreaming. Seriously, I did not have a dream that I could remember for years at a time. The reason is that alcohol reduces the REM cycle of sleep which is essential for dreaming. The shit literally steals your dreams! How evil is that? Heavy drinkers often wake up in the middle of the night because, as mentioned in the paragraph above, heavy anxiety kicks in when the alcohol is kicking out. You wake up sweating and nervous EVERY night. If you do this night after night for many years, then you become VERY tired. Being tired becomes your new reality, and you start to accept a permanent state of exhaustion. One of the biggest changes I have noticed since getting sober is the extreme state of rest that I feel. I have not felt this good since I was in my twenties. It's absolutely amazing.

Alcohol is hell on the body for sure. Since I've quit drinking, both my blood pressure and heart rate have returned to normal levels. I've had no issues with losing the feeling in the fingers of my left hand which frequently occurred after heavy drinking. My periodic gout attacks have stopped, and the uric levels in my blood are now below normal. My skin looks amazing. I have lost twenty-five pounds, have boundless energy, sleep like a rock, and no longer snore. For me, quitting drinking has been like discovering the fountain of youth!

I could go on and on about the negative effects of alcohol on the body, but I don't want to write the length equivalent of *War and Peace*. I mean, alcohol is an actual toxic poison and an extremely good one. Drinking it seriously messes you up which is completely expected. I want to switch gears and shine a light on other negative aspects of alcohol such as behavior, cost, CDC statistics, and identified health risks and diseases.

Behaviorally, it's more bad news as far as alcohol is concerned. When we drink, we are more aggressive, violent, abusive, emotional, manipulative, and risk taking. We develop extremely poor judgement and can become what seems like another person. We say and do things we would never do in our right mind. We hurt ourselves, hurt others, and isolate ourselves from friends and family so that we can drink as we please. We lie, cheat, and become about one thing in our lives — everything becomes second to the bottle. Alcohol also shuts down our coping mechanisms. Instead of developing strategies to deal with stress, depression, pain, anxiety, loss, and low self-esteem, we drink instead. I like to think of myself as having been a responsible heavy drinker, but I know that's not true. I drove my car many times when I was most certainly legally drunk. I did this alone as well as with my kids and the entire family in the car. I would never behave that way sober, but your brain on alcohol is no longer you anymore. The monster takes over. When I felt guilt or shame about this, I covered it up with more drinking.

Health and body-wise, it's more bad news. We're talking cancer of the mouth, throat, neck, esophagus, colon, breast, and liver. Anyone who speaks of the health benefits of alcohol has either been fooled or is trying to fool you. No amount is safe or beneficial. It's bad for your brain, heart, liver, and pancreas, and it weakens your immune system. You are more susceptible to pneumonia and tuberculosis and much more susceptible to infection in general. You literally can't make this up it's so bad. The CDC sums it up so well saying that long-term use of alcohol can damage every single organ in the body as well as emotional and mental health, financial status, employment, and social interactions. What the hell else is there? Combine all of this and why in the world would anyone put this inside their body? In the last years of my drinking, I often lost the feeling in three of the fingers on my left hand. Despite that obvious physical damage, I kept on drinking. This is a common occurrence with alcoholics and eventually becomes permanent. I took literally weeks to recover from any sort of cold. Since I stopped drinking, I continue to function through colds of all sorts — the minor ones from my drinking days that took me weeks to heal from no longer even slow me down. Despite global acceptance of its regular use, alcohol is among the top four most addictive drugs in the world. It's combined harm to user and harm to others rating far exceeds all other drugs. A crack or meth user is much safer to be around than a drunk. From a health perspective, complete acceptance of alcohol as a safe drug to regularly use is a big deal. It's like keeping pet alligators in the lake that you regularly swim in. Exposing yourself to that kind of risk makes no sense.

The monetary costs of alcohol to both society and individuals are unbelievably extreme. For myself, estimating ONLY the cost of alcohol, I spent $95 thousand to $150 thousand over the last twenty years. That does not include missed opportunities such as career advancement, sick days, and general poor decision making when drunk. According to the CDC, the cost of excessive alcohol use in the US alone exceeds $249 billion each year. These costs are due to lost workplace productivity, healthcare, crime and law enforcement, motor vehicle crashes and the like. These figures are underestimated because alcohol's involvement in sickness, injury, and death is not always reported. This stuff is bad and per-drink costs average $2.05 — that's insane! The damage costs inflicted by a drink are often greater than the actual cost of the drink itself. It's truly a LOSE-LOSE situation. People buy a toxin and are paying for it twice — once to drink it and a second time to repair the damage that it causes. Who pays for all this? We do. Each US taxpayer's bill for alcohol amounts to roughly $1800 per year. The true cost in human suffering is impossible to measure, but cannot be discounted — parents that have been put in jail due to DUI accidents, children taken away from parents, jobs lost, missed housing payments, cars repossessed, pain and suffering related to disease and sickness, and the daily hellish existence of the heavy drinker. That, my friends, is a TON of money that can most certainly be better spent on making a better life for yourself and your children. What would you do with your extra $1800 this year?

Finally, let's look at some sobering statistics. Alcohol is the most efficient killer that man has ever created. It is the leading cause of death worldwide with over three million alcohol related deaths globally per year. Not opioids, not cancer, not heart attacks, not car accidents, terrorists, natural disasters, or even war — just good old alcohol. Alcohol is responsible for 1 out of every 20 deaths. Nothing else compares even remotely. Its killing power has only ever been eclipsed by plagues such as the Black Death, which is estimated to have killed 50 million in 7 years. However, alcohol gives it a good run for its money and kills 21 million in that same timeframe. This pandemic-level killing power is quite shocking. How it kills you mostly depends on your age. Alcohol is the top cause of early death and disability for those under 50 mostly due to injuries such as traffic crashes, self-harm, or person to person violence. If you are over 50, alcohol related cancer, digestive disorders, or cardiovascular disease tend to get you. No amount is safe, but the more you drink, the higher your risk. I am a lucky man. If I had kept drinking for two more months, I most certainly would have been included in the over 50 digestive disorder death bucket. As it was, I could have died, but if I had been drinking the night of the emergency surgery that saved my life (and I most certainly would have), I would have been passed out and died in my sleep. You cannot overestimate the killing power of alcohol. It's just that simple.

I hope I have convinced you that Paul's assertion "Alcohol is shit." is dead-on correct. It makes us fat, sick, tired, anxious, and depressed. Alcohol steals our dreams, ages us, and makes time fly by while we are sickly down for the count. It changes our personality and makes us do and say horrible things we would never even consider sober. It costs us our health and our money both as individuals and as a society. Most seriously, it literally kills us, thousands of us, all day, every day. I didn't just pull these numbers out of the air. They were taken primarily from the CDC, WebMD, WHO, and Statista. You can check these sources and see the data for yourself. You can find an astounding amount of information on the ills of alcohol with little effort, so dig in. You will be amazed. I am just scratching the surface here, but I think I have given a pretty good overview of why alcohol sucks.

6 **MODERATION**

You think to yourself, I may have an issue with my drinking. I know. I will simply choose to drink less! Why didn't I think of this before? It's like when I was eating too much ice cream last summer and decided cut back to once per week. I got this, no problem. Or perhaps you have quit drinking and have not had a drink for months, and your dream vacation is coming up soon. You say to yourself, I've been doing great. I can drink on my vacation. I will limit myself to having only one or two drinks at dinner, and I'll be fine. Again, why didn't I try this before? How hard can it be? It seems so obvious now. We forget all about how "just stopping" has not worked in the past. That is, by the way, what we are proposing to ourselves, that we will choose to "just stop" after one or perhaps two drinks instead of our usual six to twenty.

I'm here to tell you that moderation, for anyone but the most casual of drinkers and the fact that you are reading this means you aren't one, does not work. I will tell you why in a moment, but don't just take my word for it. Many books based on scientific research have proven it. I know of some treatment programs that bill themselves as harm reduction and promote moderation as a solution. It's a shame because those of us with drinking problems so BADLY want to believe that we can still drink instead of quitting. Anyone who knows anything about alcohol obsession knows that moderation does not work.

Moderation is, in fact, the one true obsession that all problem drinkers share. I was the typical highly functional heavy drinker, and I spent many years trying to moderate my drinking. I have no doubt that, while I am telling you now that it cannot work, you will try it anyway. The issue is that this drinking problem exists entirely within our heads, and part of our brain believes that drinking alcohol is key to our survival. For this reason, we go to great lengths to preserve our drinking activity. We tell ourselves we do not have a problem and rationalize our drinking. The dream of moderation is likely responsible for most relapses. It is so easy to trick ourselves into thinking that we can pick up the bottle once again, and this time simply pour less of it into our glass. If we heavy drinkers were Superman, moderation would be our kryptonite.

For sure, everybody has tried moderation, and yet I do not know of a single person who has been able to pull it off. One of several things always happens. You either go full on back to your regular rate of drinking very quickly. Or, you do only have one or two drinks for a relatively short period of time. Then, you add one or two more drinks to your stated limit until, yeah, out of control once again. A good question is why would you even desire to have one drink? It would be frustrating and painful and far worse than not drinking at all. No, we are members of a special club of people who really like alcohol, and there is no moderation possible for us. That train pulled out of the station a long time ago back when we cared little for booze one way or the other.

Moderation is a complete fallacy, and I don't even think it's possible for casual drinkers. My wife, for example, can take or leave alcohol and only have one or two when she does drink. For that person, moderation probably could work, but there is no need for it. They have no established problem with alcohol. The concept for them makes no sense. The idea of moderation only makes sense to those that have already lost some degree of control down a one way street.

For drinkers, tolerance is the problem with moderation. We get to a level where we need a certain number of drinks to feel good and that number continually increases. It's literally a one-way street. It's sadly just how the brain works. The tolerance clock cannot be set back. Even if we stop drinking for years, we quickly pick up right where we left off. So, best case, even if we could somehow limit our drinking, we would be in constant pain because our mind knows we are holding out and teasing it, which is why efforts to moderate eventually result in full on drinking as usual. It truly is far easier to stop drinking and be at complete peace.

I always ask people why would you want to moderate? It truly is the wrong question to ask yourself. Can I choose to drink less of a highly addictive and toxic substance that is directly responsible for having caused so much pain in my life? Alcohol has brought some level of destruction to your mind, body, and soul. It's an insane proposition to want to keep consuming it.

Moderation is a natural question that any heavy drinker will consider as a solution. I did the experiment and knew moderation would not work. Once I signed myself up to quit, I realized, thank God that it doesn't work. If it did, I would still be daily killing myself at a slower pace, and I would not be living intentionally. I would still be a slave to alcohol. Being sober has brought so many benefits to my life that I would have missed out on.

While considering moderation is a good question, it is also the wrong question. A better question is what does alcohol do for you that is beneficial? Until you come to realize and accept that alcohol is a dangerous ticking time bomb toxin that is holding you back in life, moderation seems attractive. Once you educate yourself on the true nature of alcohol and how it enslaves us, you will no longer desire to drink it.

Now that I have shined a bit of light on moderation, my guess is many of you will go ahead and learn this lesson for yourself. I hope that by having read this, you will stop trying to moderate a bit sooner than you would have otherwise. The only way to freedom is to get on with omitting a daily poison from your precious life.

7 WHAT IS AN ALCOHOLIC?

I remember the first time that someone I love and respect suggested that I should consider going to an Alcoholics Anonymous meeting. I was shocked and protested "Why the Hell would I do that? I am not an alcoholic!" In my mind, AA was for drunks, people on skid row that had no pride or self-control. They were dirty, smelled of alcohol, and had no jobs. They had DUIs, parole officers and no homes. That single word 'alcoholic' brought all those images to my mind. I think most people have the same negative associations. They feel the alcoholic is someone with no self-control or self-esteem who is living in a tent under a freeway and drinking from a brown paper bag.

The reality of the situation is very different. I have been to many AA meetings and have yet to meet a single person who meets society's mental picture of an alcoholic. It's just not the case. I've been to AA members' homes, and parties, and spent countless hours with them drinking coffee, doing service work, sharing our stories, laughing together, and, in a some cases, crying together. They are people just like you and me from all walks of life and from all backgrounds. Alcohol strikes us with no preference as to who we are. Doctors, lawyers, teachers, programmers, musicians, retail workers, college students, high school students, construction workers, you name it, they are all amazing individuals and none of them conjure up the negative image that pops into most people's heads when they hear the word alcoholic.

The stigma of the word alcoholic kept me from going to AA and beginning my journey of a life without alcohol for far longer that it should have. I was too embarrassed to be seen walking into a meeting for alcoholics, and I was also afraid of the sort of people I would find there. Alcoholism is so cunning. It tells us we do not have a problem, and denial is its number one tool. We can think of dozens of reasons as to why we should keep on drinking and having to acknowledge that we must call ourselves alcoholics is high on that list. It is also part of why so many that do come to call themselves alcoholics must hit bottom so hard before they are willing to do so. They can't stomach thinking of themselves as an alcoholic and the sad fact is that belief prevents them from getting the help that they need. The stigma associated with this word is literally killing people.

I never liked the word alcoholic, but what does it really mean? Well, that depends on who is using it. When I use it, I mean anyone who wants to stop drinking but has struggled to quit. AA basically means that as well, but there is no crisp clear definition in their literature that I have found. The dictionary defines it as "someone who suffers from alcoholism", which is defined as "an addiction to the consumption of alcoholic liquor or the mental illness and compulsive behavior resulting from alcohol dependency". Even if I could find a definition that I liked, would it really matter? The definition pales in comparison to the symbolism of the word which, sadly, is of a skid row destitute foul breathed drunkard. Fighting it is like trying to change the direction of the tide. It's not easy. You are perhaps better off trying something new.

So, I have tried to find other words. The problem in creating a new word is that no one knows what you are talking about. When I use the word alcoholic in AA, everyone knows exactly what I mean. There is absolutely no confusion. I've heard many folks substitute EDR (enhanced dopamine receptor), sober warrior, or phrases like problem or heavy drinker (which I often use myself), but these cause you to either scratch your head wondering exactly what they are talking about or otherwise do not come close to capturing what AA means when they say alcoholic.

What we have here is an education problem. It's not the word. It's the fact that our society is in extreme denial of the harm that alcohol does to all of us. It's easier to throw all our fears behind the word alcoholic and ignore the problem entirely. We think "that's not us," and we go on drinking without a second thought.

I've noticed that no word which society attaches negativity to lasts for long. The word drunk seems too critical, so we use the word alcoholic. That word brings up too much baggage, so we move to the generic term addict. That word has hard drug connotations and then evolves to the phrase substance use disorder, and it goes on and on. My feeling on this is that it is a symptom of denial. We avoid confronting the addiction issues directly in front of us by instead arguing over what we should call it. We are overly careful to offend no one who doesn't already understand. The basic cause of addiction is the same no matter the substance abused, but like the word alcoholic, no one wants to be called an addict either. So, we keep making up new terms, and the general public doesn't know what we are talking about. It's denial, plain and simple. We can't even come up with an accepted word for it. For what it's worth, most in the fellowship of AA introduce themselves as an alcoholic even when they are also a drug addict. We all know that the substance we obsessed over doesn't matter, it's the recovery that counts.

I am going to continue to use the word 'alcoholic.' Quite frankly, there is no alternative that allows me to effectively communicate about "people who desire to stop drinking, but have not been able to on their own." My advice is to get over it and use the word with pride. Right now, alcoholic is a fight club word, and only those in the club truly know what it means. I drank heavily for twenty years because of denial and ignorance of the true nature of alcohol. I've come to accept that calling myself an alcoholic is a small price to pay in order to help ensure that I no longer fall into denial about my drinking. I need to face the music each day when any random thought about drinking enters my mind. The label of alcoholic helps me keep my armor up. I need its power. By owning the word and embracing the label, we can eventually redefine what it means. Society's misunderstanding is an education issue that will only be fixed by the knowledge and understanding that alcoholics are their neighbors, children's teachers, counselors, bosses, sons, daughters, and coworkers. People they love and value who are struggling with a highly addictive substance. It's a GREAT word. We just need to properly   define   it   for   others.

8 THE GRIEF OF GIVING UP ALCOHOL

Giving up drinking is much like losing a loved one. I had spent years adjusting to life with my alcoholic companion, sharing all the ins and outs of daily life for decades. For many of us, alcohol has become so ingrained into our lives that we would no more question using it than we would putting on our pants in the morning.

Saying goodbye is never easy, but for some relationships it's the only option. My old friend alcohol and I had some great, epic, times together. There is no need to deny it. Drinking alcohol was fun — perhaps some of the most fun I have ever experienced. It's hard to say goodbye to that friend, especially when you wonder how you will get along without it. However, it is important to understand that, while alcohol may seem like a standup guy, it is trying to kill us. The fair maiden I married so many years ago has become an ogre that berates me with every word. The magic is long gone, never to return. I had no choice, I had to end the bad relationship and choose to save myself.

Most who quit drinking initially feel a great loss and

wonder how they will have fun in their lives again. I know it is hard to believe at this moment, but over time as you rid your body of toxins and work to live a connected and present life, you will come to see life WITHOUT alcohol as a great opportunity, not a sacrifice. You will wonder why you waited so long to quit.

In the meantime, it helps to understand the grief process as it relates to giving up alcohol so that we may better understand the experience of saying goodbye. The accepted stages of grief are denial, anger, bargaining, depression, and acceptance.

Denial, of course, is where the alcoholic has spent most of their time until now. Perhaps decades of drinking with endless rationalizations as to why they do not have a problem. It's not our fault, but it is unfortunately how our brains react to alcohol. If you are reading this, congratulations as you have most likely ended or are, at least, open to ending your denial.

Anger comes in many forms. Perhaps we are upset or remorseful about the relationships that we have stressed or destroyed. We may have endangered or destroyed our health. We may have done things that we are ashamed to admit. We may be worn out and desperate from the daily grind of drinking too much alcohol. We wish we could go back in time to when our drinking was casual and caused no problems in our lives. We can't understand how this amazing drug that once helped us through life is now a problem for us. We have friends and loved ones who drink and have no issue at all. We may be jealous of their ability to drink, and it doesn't seem fair. Sadly, there is no turning back. There are many books that describe the now well understood process of substance addiction. It's a one-way street. We cannot unwind the clock. Once we have developed a certain level of tolerance, we will quickly reach it again if we resume drinking. Even if we have not touched a drop in many years, we start right where we left off. Our job is to get over this anger, let it go, and move on to recovering ourselves. Our heavy drinking behavior is all in the past, so we need to focus on the now and accept our new sober journey. It will be amazing, I promise you.

Bargaining for the alcoholic comes in the form of attempts at moderation. Every alcoholic that I've ever talked to has tried every strategy imaginable to control their drinking. Examples including moving to a new city, getting a new job, drinking only on the weekends, during the week, once per week, or twice per month, smoking pot instead, drinking beer instead of wine, or wine instead of whiskey, you name it, it has been tried and tried and tried again and again and again. Moderation does not work, but it is the obsession of the alcoholic. I have yet to hear of a single person who has a drinking problem that was able to moderate, not one. At best, it works for a few days, a week, or maybe a month or two, but you typically pick up, once again, right where you left off. For years I tried to moderate. I would be sober for a few days, or maybe a week to ten days and then tell myself, "You can have just one, maybe a cider." I'd drink that cider and feel pretty good about myself. An hour later I'd be thinking that another cider would be really good right now. Given that I had already proven that I can stop, I'll stop after this next one. Rolling the tape forward and many ciders later, the monster is out, and I no longer care about being sober any longer. I'm right back where I started with another turn on the heavy drinkers merry-go-round. We can spend years bargaining with ourselves about our drinking. Alcohol drives the hardest bargain around.

Depression is when we realize the reality of our situation. We have been through the moderation loop enough times, likely for two years or more, and we now

know that we cannot moderate. We understand we are in a
hole that we have created for ourselves one bottle at a
time. We often don't even enjoy drinking anymore, and it
feels more like a daily chore. We have little faith in the
future or that we can possibly stop. We may have tried
many attempts at stopping but always continued to drink.
The idea of a "last drink" seems impossible. We entertain
the idea of change, but it seems like a hopeless and
desperate task. We have reached what some call the "gift
of desperation" which means we are feeling so low,
helpless, and desperate that we are forced to accept our
reality and are now willing to do whatever it takes to
restore our peace and sanity.

Acceptance is where the magic starts to happen. We
have likely been through years of struggling through hell
with a substance that used to help us through life.
Acceptance most often occurs in a moment of clarity
where we, no longer in denial or being angry or trying to
game the system, understand we are truly in a deep
desperate hole. We now know and understand we must
change. The consequences of our drinking are no longer
tolerable to us. We have hit bottom and want, need, and
desire change.

Getting this far is HUGE. Seriously, many alcoholics
take years or even decades to get to the point of admitting
to themselves that they have a problem with alcohol. Once
we do, it opens the door to taking the first steps of
recovery. We can no longer "unsee" the problem. For
example, the day someone first attends an AA meeting
often changes them forever. They may struggle a little or
they may struggle greatly to get and stay sober. However,
they have crossed a chasm in their mind where they are
now living in reality. Things can only get better from here
on out. We can now save ourselves and have a wonderful,
healthy life. It is such a sad fact that alcohol is the leading

cause of death worldwide killing nearly three million people each year. We do not have to be one of them. We can change.

Why not write your own "goodbye letter" to alcohol right now? Tell it why you must end your relationship. Don't hold back. That bastard truly needs to know that you are done, done, done. Say things you cannot take back. Get some closure as you prepare to move on without your old   friend.

9 HOW TO BEAT CRAVINGS

Early sobriety is a struggle. I had to play to win, or I wouldn't have made it. I changed my entire schedule. I did nearly everything differently to avoid falling into past patterns. I took a different bus to work. I went in to work earlier. I went to different grocery stores where I didn't know where the alcohol was located. I stopped going to any restaurant where they even served alcohol. I turned down get-togethers with friends and colleagues. It felt a bit like playing chess. I was constantly thinking a few moves ahead in order to avoid any possible temptation. Then, one day I woke up and it magically got easier. I still had the occasional craving, but the intensity dial had been turned way down and I could readily manage them.

I wondered how this happened. I discovered Annie Grace's amazing book *This Naked Mind* and in it I found what I consider to be the answer. Prior to having read her book, I instinctively understood that there was a part of me (in my brain) that spoke to me at an instinctual level. I had no deep understanding as she describes the process, but I knew my brain was in conflict with itself about drinking. This little voice, mostly in the form of random thoughts, would make suggestions and sometimes what even felt like commands. I now understand this part of us is critical to our survival. It's the deep learned lessons that we all have ingrained into ourselves through experience. Most are helpful at keeping us alive, like when we feel that walking down a dark alley, which we've done one hundred times before, feels wrong this evening and we go around the block instead. Its job is to keep us safe and alive without getting all wrapped up in strict logical thinking. Our subconscious helps us in our daily lives by automatically relying on the long learned lessons of the past. It integrates with our conscious mind in an amazing way. Unless you are looking for it specifically, you likely don't even notice that it is happening. The conscious mind interprets the subconscious thoughts as its own, and they are seamlessly integrated. Our subconscious controls us through urges, feelings, and, yes, even cravings.

Annie's thorough research says that this is why it is so difficult to stop and stay stopped. Our subconscious mind thinks the drinking patterns of the past are critical to our survival and it loudly wishes to return to the tried and true pattern. It knows how to stop the pain, boredom, anxiety, or whatever and commands the remedy. It has our best interests at heart and thinks it is helping us to survive.

I didn't fully understand this when I quit, but I did understand that part of me was sabotaging my sobriety. Initially, I demonized that part of me. I had an angel on my shoulder but a devil in my head. I tried to resolve the cognitive dissonance by denying that part of my brain a seat at the table. That is why I struggled so. My subconscious could not be effectively ignored because it is a critical part of me. Once I changed tactics, I had much more success. Instead of trying to silence him, I told him that I loved him; but that this destructive drinking behavior is no longer working for us and needs to change.

Every day, many times per day, I thought about him and his obsession with alcohol, and told him that I loved him. I was loving the sick man because he was meeting me in the only place that he could at that moment. He was as concerned about my survival as I was, but had a completely different idea of how to ensure it. He wanted to drink because it had worked so well for so long. He ignored me for a long time. After all, he thought he was protecting my life. As I educated my conscious mind about the true destructive nature of alcohol through books, podcasts, and research, my subconscious mind eventually got the message. Without consuming a daily barrage of toxins, both my mental and physical health greatly improved, and all of this began to convince my subconscious that this new way of living was much better for my survival than my old ways.

Over time, I was able to heal that part of me. Today, he is one stone cold sober warrior. He got the message and now fights like a boss to keep me alive, but with an entirely new directive — to NOT drink. I now live my life with no desire for alcohol in the slightest. Once your subconscious is in alignment with your conscious mind, you become a stable force to be dealt with and alcohol loses all its power over you. Your subconscious is now your protector. A good friend recently prepared a special alcoholic-free drink for me. She often has them when she does not feel like consuming alcohol and was excited to share with me. I took a drink and thought that it was absolutely delicious! A citrusy, bubbly delight. After a few more sips, I had a nagging feeling that something was wrong. I felt anxious almost like I was in danger. I asked about what exactly was in the drink. It turned out that she added bitters to her alcohol-free drinks rendering them, you know, alcoholic (although very mildly). My subconscious sobriety soldier had alerted me when my conscious brain was chillin.

I believe anyone can do what I did by vigorously educating themselves about alcohol and working a spiritual journey of sobriety with others. Breaking the cognitive dissonance enabled me to stop the loop of constant cyclic drinking and to begin recovering my body and mind. We can become happier and stronger than we ever thought was   possible.

10 **HAVE A PLAN**

The secret to maintaining sobriety is having a plan. We can't wait until we are uncorking a bottle before thinking about what we will do when the strong desire to drink strikes us. We should think about it now.

In the beginning, we need a good plan and must change our entire daily routine in order to avoid temptation. Don't go to where there is alcohol and remove all alcohol from our home — full stop. For now, we must avoid going to bars with friends and any party where the purpose is to drink. Eventually we will be able to go to bars and be around alcohol again if we want to, but right now it is not an option. I stopped shopping at my regular grocery stores where I knew precisely where the alcohol was located. I got off at a different bus stop on my way home from work to avoid passing my favorite bar. I avoided Friday get-togethers with co-workers where the purpose was to drink. We can't expect to change our drinking patterns without changing our behaviors and our environment. We will have a lot of extra time on our hands now that we are no longer spending hours and hours drinking, and we don't want to be sitting around thinking about how we are not drinking. Instead, we want to be busy, busy, busy in early sobriety. We've got to replace those destructive habits with some new constructive ones. I read all that I could about addiction, and I re-engaged with my favorite hobbies. I enjoyed learning guitar, writing, reading, hiking, meeting new people, and exercise. All activities which I had given up once alcohol had taken over my life. I joined a recovery group (several actually) to connect with others who desired to change. We are unlikely to be able to quit drinking without connecting with others who are in the same boat. Believe it or not, people in recovery are the most fun and interesting people that you will ever meet. They make incredible new friends and together you can thrive in recovery.

We must plan for the time when we feel like the only thing we can possibly do is to take a drink because that is extremely likely to happen. I guarantee it. Figure out what you can do in that moment to not drink. For me, it was all about connecting with others who could give me support and talk me out of it. We do not want to power through those moments alone — we have already tried that approach. We need to ask for help. Ironically, none of us want to ask for help, but we need to get over that and just do it. Keep a few numbers on speed dial that you can call. You don't need to know the person you call all that well — just call. A conversation with someone who understands this obsession can help get us through. One place to readily get a list of numbers to call for help when you need it is at an AA meeting. A core tenant of AA is that members help each other, and many have valuable experience and are eager to share. Simply introduce yourself by first name only, and announce that you would like the numbers of anyone willing to help. By the end of the meeting, you will have an entire sheet of numbers of people who are more than willing to help in your time of need. I can't stress this enough. Trust me, talking to someone who understands the difficulties in giving up alcohol can get you past the feeling that you need a drink.

Parties, in particular, present predictable difficulties. Say that you are going to a bachelor party or maybe a wedding. Every situation is different, but you need to clearly state that you are no longer drinking. Be direct. Don't wait until someone is physically handing you a drink. In fact, it is a good idea to always have a non-alcoholic drink in your hand. All the better if it looks like a cocktail or other alcoholic drink because then no one will ask if you need a drink. It's important to make it clear to anyone who asks that we are not drinking. We think it will be a big deal, but most people just don't care if we drink or not. Don't make a big deal out of it. Casually tell them you feel so much better without alcohol and that you have given it up. Tell them the truth. Tell them nothing or everything, but tell them you are not drinking. If you don't, then they are expecting the old you to show up, and likely, whether you realize it or not, you are known as a heavy drinker. Don't fall into the trap of going in without a plan. The reality, I have found, is that people completely respect you and your decision to no longer drink. If you think about it, many of your friends probably already knew or suspected you had a problem with alcohol. If someone insists on pressuring you to drink, then that person is not any sort of friend or acquaintance you need in your life right now. Draw very clear boundaries for them; you don't owe anyone an explanation. This is your new life without alcohol. Do not under any circumstances allow someone to sabotage it.

Mentally practice what your reaction will be when someone asks you if you want a drink or, worse yet, hands you one. This happened to me at an office party when I was in my first month of giving up the grape. My company is full of highly technical people that like to party — it's part of the culture. I was always right there with them and that's exactly what they expected. My friends, not knowing that I had stopped drinking but understanding my love of booze, poured and handed me a drink. I had taken a glass so many times that accepting it was automatic. I had the glass in my hand and nearly took a sip. It was literally at my mouth before an alarm went off in my mind. I was a fraction away from starting all over once again. If I had thought about this inevitable situation before the event, I would not have been caught by surprise. Remember, no one is going to hand you a drink if they see that you already have one in your hand. Restaurants also present a unique challenge. They make a lot of money from alcohol, and the first thing they ask for is your alcoholic drink order. I always say, "No alcohol for me, thanks. What non-alcohol drinks do you have?" If I want to keep it simple, I ask for ice water, but either way I always make it clear to them that I will not be ordering alcohol. If alcohol will be served, you must think about it beforehand. This can be hard for many of us whose first instinct is to ignore any of our problems that are related to alcohol.

It's great that you are thinking about temptation now rather than waiting until you are in the middle of it! That has saved my bacon so many times. Company parties, business trips, restaurants, trips with my brothers, and even Thanksgiving dinner. So many times I had already played the scenario out in my head and had a plan of how to handle it, what to say, who to tell, and what to do if I did find myself with a drink in my hand. It's a good and essential strategy.

This sounds like a lot of work, but it really isn't. The work involved is in changing our thinking so that we are not embarrassed but actually proud of the fact that we no longer drink. Once everyone we hang out with knows this new fact about us, the pressure is off. After a short while, our defensive strategies become internalized, and we no longer think about it.

11 **A RECOVERY MINDSET**

I've been sober for some time now, and I'd like to talk about some strategies that were super helpful in achieving that. I call it having a recovery mindset because that's what recovery truly is — a change in our thinking not only about alcohol, but in how we think about ourselves. It's not like breaking a bone where the doctor fixes us up over a period of a few months and we are good to go. Recovery is a full on change in the way that we think about ourselves and our life. The alcohol part of that equation was how we were surviving, and the trick of recovery is to learn to survive on our own by replacing that coping mechanism with one that is sustainable and supports our lives. This process will take some time. It starts by stopping drinking and continues with an amazing journey of self-discovery and true happiness.

The idea is to change our thinking from one of "I am sacrificing without alcohol" to thinking that we are giving ourselves the amazing gift and opportunity of sobriety. In order to do that, we must first see alcohol for what it truly is. That knowledge came to me through education and repetition. I educated myself about addiction, alcohol, and recovery and then I practiced new ways of thinking through the connections of friends, recovery groups, and writing about my experiences. There are so many ways discussed here in this book and elsewhere that can be used to change your relationship with alcohol. All it takes is consistent effort. My most difficult day juggling my life while also making time to get to a meeting and connecting with others is far easier than it ever was struggling with alcohol on a daily basis.

In the beginning, I thought that I simply needed to drink less. Then I learned that I cannot drink less, so I thought that I just needed to stop drinking. Then I learned that while I no longer drank, all the reasons why I drank were still there. Then I started a spiritual journey to recover my true self, and live in the present moment so that I no longer felt the desire to drink. I am recovered from drinking as I no longer need to drink, but I will be recovering by finding better and happier ways to live for the rest of my life. At a year sober my wife asked me if I was recovered. I thought about it and told her that I no longer have a drinking problem, but I'm sure that I can find one very quickly. I am at peace, but it took many years of proving to myself that I actually do suck as drinking. It's a hard-learned lesson for me that I can never drink again without risking all that is most important to me.

This is the irony of alcohol. We start to drink as a way to solve our problems in facing reality. Maybe it's stress, anxiety, or some sort of pain that feels unbearable without alcohol. After some time, the alcohol stops working and drops us on the pavement so to speak. The pain of that bottom causes us to begin the process of recovery which leads to a new life for ourselves. It's a weird cycle where alcohol first solved all our problems, then caused all our problems, and then as a side effect once again solved all our problems but this time through its absence.

We have lived our entire lives in a society that worships alcohol. It will take some time to reverse the damage in our programmed thinking, so be patient. Once we do, however, we will have no desire for alcohol and no more obsession. We will no longer think about it for days, weeks, and months on end. We are programmed to drink in our society almost from birth. To stop, we need to deprogram ourselves by replacing that positive association with the negative one that it deserves. I've come to believe this is the only way to quit for good — to both consciously and subconsciously understand that alcohol is a toxin that must be avoided entirely. It's like a snake — perfectly safe for you to be close to, just don't let it touch you.

Getting sober is very much a mental process. Once you are detoxed, your physical body is no longer dependent. For most of us, that takes only a few days. At that point, our addiction is all wrapped up in that bone prison sitting atop our heads. It does not exist in the physical world, but is a mental construction. This makes it both easier and harder to resolve. We can't cut it out like a bad appendix. We've got to change our thinking.

I remember key turning points in life when I decided to be different. Just up and decided, quite consciously, that I am going to redefine myself. College, my first professional job, my marriage, and my first child were all pivotal times in my life. At those key moments, I thought I am changing right now. Everything before is going to be different from everything after. Take college, for example. In high school, things were easy for me academically. When I started college, the academics were very challenging. I decided to become a different person, one who studied and was a true student of learning. I consciously modified my behavior (becoming an excellent student) until it became second nature. I watched as others who were already doing this were successful, and I befriended them and asked questions. I became the company that I kept. I came to enjoy my new self as I knew that I was building not only my future, but a new me that had a thirst to understand all my studies. I gave myself to it and was far happier than before. My education was not a sacrifice of my freedom to be a carefree teen, but a privilege and opportunity to become whatever I wanted to become. In short, I had changed my thinking forever by consciously reprogramming myself for the better. I believe this is also how I stopped drinking.

I put in the time. I worked hard. I was dedicated to becoming the new me. My journey became part of the reward. I enjoyed redefining and discovering new things about myself. I tried new things, read different books, went out of my way to challenge being in my comfort zone, connected with people completely different from myself, and explored anything that I thought could help me. I fell in love with my new life without alcohol and that made it easy. I think deprogramming your thinking from one of sacrifice to one of opportunity is key. Willpower alone will only get us so far. It's not enough to only stop drinking. We don't want a life of suffering through sobriety constantly lusting for a drink. We will take that tension out on all those around us as well as ourselves. Life will be a chore like Sisyphus pushing the boulder up the hill, unable to appreciate the beauty of the hillside. It's better to take away the strength we have previously given alcohol and flip our thinking about both alcohol and ourselves.

How exactly do you do this? I wish I could give a set of step-by-step directions, but it doesn't work that way. There are so many variables in a person's life that leads them to become addicted to alcohol. There is no one factor that neatly explains this compulsion and ties it up in a bow.

Similarly, there is no step-by-step prescription to set it all right again. There can't be because the true reasons that you drink need to be resolved within your conscious and subconscious minds and that process will be different for each of us. There is an answer, however. There are many programs that give us the opportunity to resolve the unique issues that are causing us to drink in the first place. Most of them, or at least the most popular ones that I am aware of, allow us the opportunity to take a spiritual journey to get to know and repair ourselves with a new awareness that we have never dreamed possible. For this to work, however, we have to want it for ourselves. For example, you can get a driving under the influence citation (DUI) and a judge can send you to a twenty-eight-day detox and perhaps a few months of an intensive outpatient program (IOP). All of these are excellent opportunities to start turning yourself around, but you have to want to change. Anyone can learn the tools from AA, Refuge Recovery, or IOP and have everything they need to stay sober and rebuild their lives. If you don't want it, however, then all you are doing is learning the tools. For these programs to work effectively, you really do need a desire to quit, seek help, and take action. We cannot think our way out of a drinking problem. Even if you don't have a strong desire to stop at the moment, I suggest you try anyway. I've known many who used the "fake it until you make it" strategy of continuing to go to meetings while they struggled to stop. Eventually, they had enough and were ready to finally stop. By that time, they had met enough friends in recovery who were able to give them the help and support they needed.

If there is one key thing to remember, it is that you will not be able to do this alone. Initially this is probably the last thing you want to hear. I struggled alone for so many years, and it was the loneliest that I have ever felt. My heavy drinking was done alone and secretly. Many of us hit our drinking bottoms in isolation. We cut ourselves off from those who we felt were a threat to our drinking, or we came to the realization that it's easier to drink alone. Being alone and a heavy drinker is dangerous when you are trying to quit. We've proven that to ourselves so many times already. To recover, get with like-minded people and outside of your comfort zone. It seems like a risk, but you will be so glad that you put yourself out there and connected with those that fully understand your situation. You can't do it alone. We are a strong and stubborn bunch — survivors, headstrong, filled with denial, and often a lack of concern for our health or comfort. For most of our lives, that has worked, but it will not work for overcoming this obsession. Get outside your comfort zone and connect with others for strength and accountability. You will thank me for it. You may not need the help of others forever, but in my experience, everyone does for at least the first year of sobriety. You have nothing to lose and everything, including some amazing new friends, to gain.

Here is the playbook that I used to get sober. You can use it to help create your own. Whenever I felt that pull to drink or felt lost as to what to do next, I would look at this list and TAKE ACTION. Doing things is how I got passed this.

- Start Today — don't wait, go all in, work on it daily no matter what and you will make progress
- Don't Do It Alone — accept that I need help
- Choose to Stop — convince myself that I really want to quit and that moderation is a myth, apply this not only to drinking, but any aspect of my life that is not adding value to it
- Go to AA (or similar) — I can't do it alone, I need the help of others
- Education — learn about addiction, alcohol, recovery groups, meditation, a new hobby,

anything that can help
- Get Spiritual — check my ego, feel my emotions, and help others
- Change — get out of my comfort zone, do new things, meet new sober people
- Live in the now — forget about yesterday and don't worry about tomorrow, my job is to be me right now and to think only about today
- Have a plan — stay stopped by mitigating triggers, don't walk into a lion's den of alcohol unprepared
- Meditate — hypnotherapy and meditation reprogram my subconscious mind to no longer desire alcohol and are an excellent coping mechanism for daily stress
- Stay Connected — daily communication with those fighting the same battle keeps me on track
- Live Your Life — connect with old friends and family, dream, write a book, publish an app in the app store, hike all over, help others when I can — all instead of drinking.
- Keep a Journal — remember where I came from, where I am, and where I want to go

12 WHAT TO EXPECT AT AN ALCOHOLICS ANONYMOUS MEETING

I've been attending meetings for some time now. In the beginning, I was nervous about going to AA. I had no idea what to expect or how it worked. I was worried that someone would ask me to speak, but I was unsure of what I would even say. I'm an introvert and was uncomfortable sharing and speaking with such a large group of people. It turns out that my concerns were unfounded. No one made any demands of me of any sort. I sat and listened for the first month, and didn't say a word. I learned a lot in that time.

The first thing about meetings is that, while the venue varies wildly, most are held in churches of various denominations. If you are agnostic, don't let that bother you. No religion is pushed although there is much discussion of a higher power, and for most people I've met, they label that power God. I've been to bonfire meetings, meetings in office buildings, meetings in old hotels, and meetings in strip malls — they are everywhere! No one is officially in charge, and there is no bureaucracy, leadership, fees, political affiliation, causes, or fund raisers.

The participants create the environment which leads to different vibes for different meetings. It always amazes me how people create varying social environments simply by being there. No two meetings are the same, and yet they are also quite similar. There is only a single requirement to attend, and that is that you have a desire to stop drinking.

For those who haven't been to a meeting, the format is pretty much the same at most of the meetings that I've attended. Generally lasting an hour to an hour and a half, the meeting is initiated by the meeting chair with a brief introduction of the agenda for the evening. Nothing surprising, it's usually a few announcements, an inspirational reading likely from the Big Book, a speaker or two, open sharing, donations, and that's a wrap. The chair often starts by asking if there are any visitors from out of town or those who are within their first thirty days of sobriety. If so, those people may introduce themselves by first name only (it's anonymous) saying something like, "Hi, my name is Tom. I'm an alcoholic and haven't had a drink for twelve days". The meeting then always begins by reading the twelve steps and traditions. After that, a preselected person reads a passage from the Big Book which deals with the discussion topic of the evening. This person is most often the first speaker and shares how the passage relates to their experience. There is always lots of coffee and it's generally good (but no guarantees there). It's the only mind-altering substance endorsed and recovering alcoholics have figured out how to make it quite well.

Let me just say that sharing is an amazing experience. Alcoholics, in general, are excellent story tellers and good all-around bullshitters with dramatic life experiences. Humor is often a big part of someone's share, and there is often so much laughter that it feels like a frat party without the drugs and alcohol. Some of the stories that I've heard have deeply touched me and made me laugh, think, cry, get motivated — you name it, you'll hear it. The shares most often have to do with the evening's topic and should be less than five minutes, but there are no hard rules. No one is going to judge or criticize you.

The big difference that I have noticed in various meetings concerns how sharing is done. In small groups, they go around the circle giving each person a chance to share although you are always free to pass. In larger groups, the chair usually selects those to speak mostly from the pool of people that they know as part of the home group, but also occasional newcomers. After these called shares, there is an open period where anyone can share. I've also been to meetings where people self-select by standing up and sharing one at a time. No matter how the speaker is selected, there is no cross talk. In other words, you listen to the speaker — no questions or intentional communication with them at all. If you feel compelled to talk to someone who has shared, you can privately approach them after the official meeting is over. Sharing is the bulk of the meeting. My thinking has been profoundly changed by the stories of people with twenty-eight years of sobriety as well as by those who have less than thirty days. Everyone benefits everyone else through their shares.

About half-way through the meeting, a collection plate is passed for donations in order to pay for the coffee, rent the room, and buy the Big Book for someone who cannot afford it. We're talking a couple bucks here, no one makes any money off of this. The plate is also a chance for attendees to get their attendance slips signed. Some are on parole or there from rehab specifically for the meeting and are required to prove that they were attending. In my regular meeting, there are always plenty of newcomers. I live in a large city, and there is no shortage of alcoholics and addicts who have come to realize that they need help.

While AA started out for alcoholics, the reality is that most alcoholics today have been "drinking and drugging". We call ourselves alcoholics or addicts, but I don't get too caught up on the drug of choice. It's the same brain mechanism and twelve step program to free yourself. There is an A for every drug — NA (narcotics), MA (marijuana), HA (heroin), SA (sex), etc. — so many meetings.

At the end of the meeting, announcements related to AA, upcoming events, requests for volunteers, sponsees, etc. are read. The meeting is then officially ended often with the Serenity Prayer (agnostics please search and replace 'God' with 'higher power') and then involves everyone pitching in to fold and stack the chairs.

After the meeting, people enthusiastically meet outside in the designated smoking area in order to, of course, smoke and chat. It's a great opportunity to really get to know others. I don't smoke, but I never miss this time to deeply connect with others. In the beginning, I always avoided the after-meeting chats, but I highly recommend them. It always amazes me how different we alcoholics are, but we are also the same. All walks of life are there — doctors, lawyers, construction workers, teachers, judges, baristas, homeless people, young people, old people, college students, tattoo covered, some wearing bow ties, all races, colors, creeds, and sexual orientations. You name it and you will see it. Some of us need a tune-up and some of us need a full rebuild. We are all different, but we are also the same. The thing that ties us together is the accepting support we give each other in working a program to help ourselves and each other. It's truly magical for those two hours and it has changed my life.

Once I became comfortable going to meetings, I started to feel at home. I met people, learned their names, and grew to know them from their shares and by talking with them after the meeting. You get to know many details of their personal lives — their struggles, their triumphs, their strengths and weaknesses. You become friends. You come to know them at a deep level that rarely happens in everyday life. This is raw, no bullshit, direct and honest communication. It binds you together, and you can't help but care for and love many of those you meet. Through this process, you also share and heal yourself as well as your new friends. What happens in those rooms is nothing short of miraculous.

I hope I have given you some idea of what a typical AA meeting looks like. If you are considering attending a meeting, I strongly encourage you to do so. AA has been one of the most incredible experiences of my life. There are so many meetings all day every day, and all you have to do is find one that feels right to you. If you commit to going for one month, you may find that the experience changes your life forever.

13 RECOVERING ALCOHOLICS ARE FUN!

My home group is a fun-loving group of people. A typical meeting sounds more like a party with all the laughter, smiling, and people doing the wave for momentous events, like someone hitting a year of sobriety or a visitor from somewhere special. It's like a great party from back in my drinking days, only there is no alcohol.

Recently a visitor commented during her share that she takes her sobriety very seriously and was having a hard time feeling comfortable with all the laughter and joy she observed during the meeting. This woman was no stranger to AA. She was eight years sober. Her comment reminded me of how I felt when I first started coming to AA and this meeting in particular.

It took me quite a few runs at it before I started to regularly attend AA meetings. In fact, for my first meeting attempt, I never even entered the building! I would drive to the church, park my car, and then sit in the parking lot as I watched others show up and walk into the building. When people stopped coming, I would start the car and drive back home. I just couldn't do it. I was scared for many reasons, but the big thing for me was that going inside meant I would finally be admitting to myself that I had a problem and needed help. I'm sure that this is common for many newcomers. It takes a lot of guts to walk into those rooms for the first time when you have no idea what goes on in there.

One night, I had gone two weeks without drinking, which was about as long as I could go without starting again. I decided to drive to the liquor store and celebrate my two weeks with a few bottles as I had done so often in the past. I got in the car and headed to the grocery store when a funny thing happened. I pulled up to a stop sign preparing to make a left and glanced at the clock in the car. I saw that it was eight o'clock and a Wednesday, which just happened to be the start time of the closest meeting to my house. In that instant, instead of a left, I took a right and drove to the AA meeting that I had yet to actually attend. It was odd. It was pure coincidence that it was both eight o'clock and a Wednesday, but perhaps it was my still unknown-to-me higher power at work.

I was determined! This time, when I got to the church, I parked my car and confidently walked directly into the building. I was about fifteen minutes late. I was shocked when I walked in — so much laughter, smiles, and arm waving going on. I initially thought I had walked into the wrong room! Here I was in deep despair trying to quit drinking and it sounded like a busy beer hall on a Saturday night. I walked in, sat down, and listened to the members as they shared their stories, and the most amazing thing happened. As I listened to those stories, I suddenly realized that these people, although they were completely different from me in most respects, were the same as me in their relationship with alcohol. I had never before met anyone who was like me. All my life I had assumed I was somehow unique, and I now found myself in a room with sixty people who were just like me. I had found my people and it was a tremendous relief.

So, I started to regularly attend meetings but continued to struggle with how I felt about all the joy and laughter expressed there. It seemed wrong to me that such serious matters were often shared with laughter. It was almost at times like locker room talk where we bragged about size, scars, or injuries — people one-upping one another with shocking stories of their past (particularly after the meetings during smoking time outside). I just didn't get it.

One time after returning home from a meeting, my wife asked me how it went, and I described my confusion. I told her the meetings seemed too joyous to me given the serious nature of why we were all there! I thought about this for a long time.

One night I awoke from a terrible nightmare. I am horribly afraid of heights and basically most any ride you might see at a fairground. My daughter, however, loves roller coasters and I force myself to face my fears and ride with her whenever she asks. She's a teenager and I realize it will not be long before she stops asking me so often as our relationship changes and she starts her own life journey. In this nightmare, we were riding a large roller coaster — looping, swooping, up and down, lurching through turns at breakneck speed. I woke up covered in sweat.

The second I awoke, I immediately understood that AA meetings are like roller coasters! Roller coasters are meticulously engineered by smart people with advanced degrees and years of study in physics, engineering, construction, and safety. As horrifying as those rides can be, they are absolutely safe (you know, for the most part). Because deep down we know that they are safe, that also makes them fun. We allow ourselves to scream and laugh in both fear and joy because we know we are safe from any harm. A good roller coaster ride makes me feel 100 percent alive. Once it's over, that is!

AA meetings are the same way. The reason we can share our pain is because we know we have a solution to our problems through our program of acceptance, meetings, fellowship, steps, a sponsor, and service. We have an answer, and we know we are safer than we have been in a long time. We can laugh, joke, and jeer about our darkest thoughts and past experiences because we know we now have a way to live our lives. We can throw all our feelings out on the floor while sharing because we know we are among peers and no one will judge or criticize us. We feel safe. I finally understood and was able to celebrate our raucous meetings because I got it. The laughter we often hear in AA meetings means that those meetings are working.

14 RELAPSE - HAVE A LIFELINE

Relapse can be as serious as a heart attack. When we let the monster loose, hard core drinkers are not at all sure what he may do or how long he may rampage. For most people trying to quit drinking, relapse will be a part of the process. While it may be inevitable for many, it should be avoided because the risk of self-harm or harm to others is very real.

I meet many young men in recovery when I visit a local sober living home. Their setup is three men to a townhouse in a group of six town houses. They are amazing people — so inspiring, many of them young and in their twenties, putting their lives back together. It also seems like an all-day every day AA meeting. These guys share their past and their struggles with each other, and they bond quickly.

The rules are fairly simple including one that says that if you relapse and fail regular random drug and alcohol tests, then you are out. Officially, you get three days to pass the drug test again, but in reality, the guys that do relapse quickly drop off the map. It's a sad time because everyone knows it could have been them. Most of these young men were addicted to hard drugs in addition to alcohol which can be very dangerous when you relapse. It's all too easy to start with a few drinks and then move on to your drug of choice.

Guys come and go as they progress in their recovery and get their lives back. They get jobs, go back to school, attend counseling and meetings, and eventually are ready to live again on their own. Many remain friends after they move on from sober living and visit their buddies regularly at the houses. It's a brotherhood and community in every sense.

Last summer, a young man, who had graduated from the houses some time ago and visited regularly, had a relapse. He had been drinking and was driving under the influence. He happened to be driving on a long bridge when he was stopped by the police, pulled over to the shoulder, and hand-cuffed at three in the morning. In his intoxicated state and facing jail time, he made a run for it and jumped off the bridge. He hit the water and drowned.

This sad story is a lesson that relapse can have serious unintended consequences that far outweigh a sobriety date reset. Everyone needs a few phone numbers that they can call anytime of the day or night. Connecting with someone before we have that first drink could save a life.

If you do relapse, keep in mind that it is not the end of the world. In fact, for most people, it is part of the process. A friend of mine known as Cafe Jim in one of my recovery groups once described quitting as like chopping down a tree. You swing the axe again and again until the final cut makes the tree fall. The final swing was no more or less important than all the previous ones. They all contributed equally to cutting down the tree. The last swing was simply the one that finally got the job done. Sobriety and getting sober are like that for many. You may relapse, but if you get back up and keep at it, you will eventually have your last drink when the tree finally falls. The only way to lose this battle is to stop trying.

15 MY HIGHER POWER STORY

I've always been a lazy seeker and an extreme doubter of anything that I cannot directly see, touch, or measure. I have a scientific mind, and while I cannot rule out the existence of God, I chose to not think too much about the unprovable for most of my life.

Two months after I decided to stop drinking, I had emergency surgery to remove a large section of my intestine that had died. I was in pretty bad shape. It's a serious thing to have a dead organ in your body. I could have died and the pain was the most excruciating I have ever felt.

At its worst, the pain was so severe I could feel my sanity slipping away. After several hours of tests while the doctors were trying to determine what was wrong, the pain meds stopped working altogether and I was in a very bad place.

When the pain moved to my back as well as my stomach, I entered a new plateau of hell that I didn't think was possible. I gave up all hope at that point and accepted that I was going to die. I wanted the pain to stop and would have done anything to make it go away. At this point, I could no longer talk, but I was mostly aware of what was going on around me. I squeezed my wife's hand and tried to say goodbye, but I could no longer speak. They moved me to the operating room and were preparing to cut me open. They had done all their tests and still had no solid conclusions. I was failing fast, and they needed to take some drastic action right away.

As the next wave of intense pain hit me, it was like a light switch suddenly had turned on. Time stopped, the pain stopped, my thinking cleared, and I could breathe again. I was being held by this beautiful blue light, and it was the most calm and serene experience I've ever felt, like a small child being held by its mother while it slept. There was no speech between us, just this overwhelming sense of love, acceptance, calm, and warmth. The light was not holding the physical me but my soul, thoughts, and feelings. It was like I had been run through a filter and all the damaged and painful parts of me were still stuck down in my physical body. This was the purest form of myself. All my pain, fears, anxiety, worldly concerns and my addiction were left behind in my physical body. I basked in this light completely overwhelmed and calmed by it.

After a short time, I began to think of my body and its pain and how bad off it was at the moment. I became concerned and bothered that my time was over. I didn't want to die. I still had things to do and people that I love and want to help. I thought of everyone in my life that needed me and I felt a great sorrow for abandoning them. I became extremely desperate and did not know what to do.

The light conveyed a single thought to me at that moment — "Give it all to me." All that I had to do was give away all my worldly concerns and problems to this great power to take on, and I could be relieved. In that moment, I was turning myself over to this power, and I was willing to accept any outcome, including my own death. So, I gave it all away, and felt my soul fill with love, and that's the last thing I remember.

I woke up a day later, spent a week in the hospital afterwards, and made an amazing recovery. The doctors were astounded at my mental positivity and energy towards my physical recovery. I know it sounds crazy — trust me, I was the biggest doubter of any sort of God, but I can't deny my experience or the changes that have happened since then.

I had been sober for over two months when this happened, but it had not been easy due to a smoldering desire for booze. I was constantly on the lookout to avoid any situation where I would be tempted and have access to alcohol because I knew that my resolve was weak. After my experience, I had no need for alcohol in the least — no craving, no more desire, no more drinking dreams. It was just gone. My higher power did that for me, and I will be eternally grateful. I have a new lease on life, and I need to honor this second chance that I have been given and to help others who need it.

That's my higher power story, and for what it's worth, it has made a believer out of me. I'm not sure that it's enough to simply want God in your life. At least, it wasn't for me, I had to truly need God. I needed to get to the point where I surrendered and was willing to turn my life over. Once I accepted my higher power, everything has been easier.

16 **ARE WE CRAZY?**

Are we crazy? Not laughing in a corner crazy, but driven by some invisible force not completely under our control that we must learn to harness crazy.

I was recently talking with a mother whose daughter is using drugs. She had so many questions wanting to know all the reasons why. Sadly, there are no answers although any parent will lose many sleepless nights trying to find some. I've come to think that having the mental wiring that predisposes someone to becoming an addict is just the luck of the draw. I've been down this road before trying to explain the feeling of addiction. You can't fully describe the unstoppable compulsion to drink or use drugs to someone who has never felt that insane pull. 'Just stopping' doesn't work. It's a hard conversation. They blame themselves and can't understand that you can't help someone that doesn't want it. They want to understand and treat addiction like they do any other classified disease, but it's the only one that tells you that you are not sick.

I explained to her as best as I could what addiction feels like. At one point she said, "That sounds absolutely crazy." Not much argument there, destroying yourself with drugs and alcohol is undeniably insane. We use alcohol to treat the pain so that we can keep going. It seemed like a great solution at the time. A solution to a problem we didn't even know that we had and could not articulate. Some element of psychic trauma to forget that makes us behave in ways that most would describe as crazy.

Even after quitting and during recovery, I think most addicts march to a different drum. Now that I am looking for it, we just think differently. Crazy like a fox dedicated to something we love. For myself, my life has been full of one total obsession to something that was important to me after the next, particularly for things that I enjoyed. Extreme dedication that pretty much took over everything. Most of those things added value to my life or, at least, didn't threaten to destroy it, but alcohol threatened to wrap it all up and call it a day. It ended my insane drive but at the cost of making me care about nothing but alcohol. I cured my craziness by becoming sick.

Learning to accept and leverage the less controllable part of my nature has been so amazing in sobriety. I can now use my "damn the torpedoes" mentality that allowed me to ignore the difficulties in my life while drinking all those years for good. So, yes, I'm glad that I'm crazy. It's my superpower.

17 THE INSANITY OF ALCOHOL

They say that one drink is too many and a thousand is not enough. When I first started drinking, one was never enough but three was just about right. The problem was that, over the years, three turned into four, five, six, and so on until I was often drinking three bottles of red wine at a go. Still, I kept going, despite all the pain from hangovers, missed days of work, and failed commitments. I felt like hell most every morning.

It wasn't until I began having negative physical symptoms lasting for days that I started to consider that perhaps I should seriously look at my drinking habits. I would occasionally lose the feeling on some of the fingers of my left hand. I knew it was alcohol related because it only happened when I had been hitting the bottle hard. Despite knowing that I was causing nerve damage, I still kept on drinking for another two years. I remember when I first told my wife about these symptoms, although I did not tell her about the amount of alcohol I was drinking. I always hid that from the family. Of course, she told me to go to the doctor. I took her advice — nine months later! By this time, the problem had escalated from very occasional to very often.

I went to the doctor, and when he eventually got around to asking me about how much alcohol I drink, I flat-out lied to him admitting only to 'a few drinks after dinner'. The crazy thing is I somehow told myself that I had tried resolving this problem with a good effort despite my lying. I told myself nothing could be done, so I kept on drinking. I accepted having numb fingers like I had accepted my daily drinking of alcohol. It was now a part of my daily life. I continued on this path of self-harm for close to another year before I hit bottom from my heavy drinking. It's a miracle that I have feeling in those fingers today.

This is the nature of alcohol. It makes us act in an insane manner where we can easily ignore the obvious evidence of how it is destroying us. It is utter madness.

18 WHY I DRANK

There is no single compelling reason that I can convey for why I drank so much for so long. I just did. For a long time, I simply liked it, and then it became a daily habit. I drank normally for nearly fifteen years, where I could take it or leave it, and alcohol rarely entered my thoughts. I continued to drink a highly addictive substance and, quite predictably, became addicted. I had an amazing childhood, incredible parents, good friends, and a wonderful college experience. My career has always gone extremely well, and I am married to a loving wife and have two wonderful children. I thought my drinking situation was unique or special. We all do, and we are right. No two roads into addiction or out of it are exactly the same although there are so many similarities.

I think most of us drink because of past trauma. Like alcoholism, trauma is a broad sliding scale. Trauma can be meteoric, such as a parent dying, physical, emotional, or sexual abuse, parental neglect, an injury, etc. Trauma can also be something far more subtle such as being overly shy, having a bad break up, being publicly shamed, being ignored, or not making the football team. These events, objectively big or small, mold our internal thinking about ourselves. Many alcoholics internalize these feelings into low self-worth or self-hatred. We may insist that we are fine when we are far from it because we don't want to be a bother. How we cope with and react to our trauma makes all the difference. I can be extremely resilient in one area and very fragile in another. There is no rhyme or reason. It's just how we are. Growing up, I had issues with self-confidence, wanting to fit in, and pleasing people — feelings that are common to many people. People often effectively cope with painful experiences in a healthy way in that they accept it, let it go, or work to bring about changes that make the situation acceptable; but some of us internalize specific traumas. We may use alcohol as the coping mechanism for the pain and may not even consciously remember the trauma over time. The numbing effects of alcohol become our solution to our problems. I grew up poor and despite being happy and well cared for, I resented this to my core. I hid most of my private life from my classmates at school and I carried that behavior on into college and beyond. The shame of my background started in grade school when a classmate teased me about my clothes, my appearance, and where I lived. From that point on, I became an actor in order to hide my true self from the world because I wanted to be accepted. I trained myself to be an imposter and a people pleaser. I wanted to fit in and be accepted. Later in life, these skills came in handy in my professional life as a highly functional alcoholic because I was accustomed to only showing others what I wanted them to see. I could control my exposure in any situation. My approach to life and dealing with its inevitable problems was changed by a traumatic experience that the child version of me had experienced. Did this trauma contribute to my drinking later on? Absolutely! It was one of the factors, but there are so many variables. There are so many gray areas in trying to figure out the answer to "why?" The same obsessive thinking that helped lead to my reliance on alcohol was also the same compulsion that propelled my career. It was both a strength and a weakness. It is simply how I am made and I couldn't have been any other way. I still have feelings of not belonging today, but I have adapted to be able to deal with them in a functional way.

I have no darkness, no void, and no large broken pieces that need mending. Nothing haunts me — I'm generally not critical of myself or others, don't often get angry, and have few regrets, but I still need to be healed. I think that we all do to some degree. The twelve steps of AA can work for anyone — you could be a drunk on the street or Mother Theresa. We can all improve our spirituality. I continue to work them, by myself and with others. They have brought me so much inner peace. I have learned so much about myself in sobriety, and it is the most amazing thing that I have ever done. Spirituality has given me so many gifts and has made me far stronger than I ever knew that I could be. It took me a long time to discover that I couldn't think my way out of this problem by magically discovering all the reasons why I drank. There are many reasons and understanding some of them only came when I had taken action to deal with those feelings in my daily life. It's just more of the insane nature of how addiction works. I could only understand my reasons for drinking once I had mitigated and dealt with them. If you want to understand why you drink, my advice is to take action to connect with others making a similar spiritual journey, and the why will magically present itself over time. Don't cause yourself additional anxiety today by constantly searching for that leprechaun's pot of gold. You'll find it when you stop looking. When I finally stopped drinking, I started to come to know some of the reasons as to why I drank, but it took a long time working on my recovery. I am still learning more about myself all the time.

I drank heavily for over twenty years and finally stopped drinking one day, and that was it for alcohol and me. All that drinking had made my body and soul very tired. I first needed to recover physically, then mentally, and finally spiritually. I continue to make progress in each of these areas as long as I completely avoid the snake oil that is alcohol. My relationship with alcohol has changed at this point, and it will never be a part of my life again. If I ever drink again it will be because I forced myself to do so.

I've rediscovered my higher power as part of my recovery, and that gives me comfort. I gave up on God decades ago because I simply didn't see much evidence of God's presence in the world. The rooms of AA are amazing to me. I see God there at every meeting in the magic of connection, understanding, compassion, and support. People with addictions helping others among them is one of the most beautifully human things that I have ever been a part of. So much compassion, support, vulnerability, and honest communication is incredibly healing. It's a spiritually enriching solution. Looking back, I could say that a general lack of spirituality led to my problems.

So, there you have it. I don't fully understand all the reasons why I drank so much, not really, not yet. I regularly make new connections about myself and why I drank. There have been many reasons. I honestly had to work hard at becoming addicted to alcohol, and it took me many years. However, once the switch was flipped, I was living on borrowed time, and alcohol, the patient killer of life, had my number. I understand the reasons that made me decide to stop, but not the path that got me there. In the end, I don't need to fully understand. I am just so grateful to be sober for TODAY.

19 CHRISTMAS IN A BOTTLE

Christmas night was always a long night of drinking for me. My wife and kids always went to bed early after we got home from the evening or late-night church service, and then I went to work.

First, I would open a nice bottle of red wine, and then I would begin pulling out the presents, wrapping them, and placing them under the tree. Many presents required assembly, and that made for a long night. I would continuously drink during the entire wrapping and assembly process, would finish the first bottle in the first hour, and open a second which took a bit longer. After the second hour and the second bottle, I was done with wrapping and only had the detailed assembly to work out. This often took longer than expected as I was several bottles in, but I was always persistent as I worked on bottle number three. Some years, I was up quite late into the night — being alcoholic Santa was hard work.

By the next morning, I was not in the best of shape but

would manage to drag myself out of bed and join in the festivities with the rest of the family that was 'bright-eyed and bushy-tailed' as usual. I took a nap mid-morning and was in decent shape before the company arrived early afternoon. It was an extremely long day most years.

As the kids got older, things got better. I would always drink as I wrapped and placed the presents under the tree even though they no longer believed in Santa. It, like my drinking, had become customary. Unlike when they were younger, there was nothing to assemble anymore, so I drank a bit less and was in better shape the next morning. However, I was always hung over to some degree.

This will be my first year in probably twenty years that I have been Santa stone-cold sober. LaCroix has replaced Merlot in my life, and I could not be happier. I am looking forward to enjoying the full Christmas Day tomorrow and being present for each moment with my family.

20 I CRY AT MEETINGS

I've got a confession. I cry at AA meetings. I used to be embarrassed about it, but I have recently changed my perspective. I am not talking full on, hands over my face, sobbing, but my eyes would most definitely get very moist. In the man's manual of life, it's crying. No one in my professional or personal life would believe it. I am a stable guy who remains cool under pressure. At five months into being sober, however, my emotions often tended to get the best of me. After giving it some thought and taking a good look at my struggles in giving up alcohol, I had an epiphany. I'm trying to save my life here! That can certainly get emotional at times. If I shed a few tears, who cares? Hell, it feels good. Without the constant numbing effect of alcohol in my daily life, I am always in the present moment, and that entails happiness, sadness, delight, disappointment, wonder — you name it, and I'm feeling it. In short, I am fully living my life, and that, dear friends, is an emotional undertaking. It will take some time for my mind to readjust to its new chemical environment free of toxins.

Recently my daughter asked me if I wanted to see a

movie. I take advantage of this as often as I can. She is fifteen, and I know that all too soon, hanging out with Dad will become increasingly rare. Those teenage years go by in a flash, and I honestly don't even care what we do. The point, for me, is to have fun with my daughter. She suggested *A Star is Born* which, quite honestly, I was not excited about. I was assuming that, like many remakes, this one was likely to be a poor effort, and my expectations were quite low. But, as I said, I was happy to spend a fun evening with my daughter, rehashed movie or not.

I couldn't have been more wrong! *A Star is Born* is nothing short of amazing. The music, the direction, the acting, the story, it's all incredibly well done. I'd go so far as to call it a new masterpiece. I will tell you, however, that as a recovering alcoholic, it will rip your heart out. As the story unfolds, you watch, you remember, and you think about what alcohol does to you. I've never seen a movie that depicts the struggles and pain of addiction as well as this one. It was very emotional. Addiction is the unseen third main character whose presence, like in real life, is felt in every scene. As I left the theater with my daughter, I was not only drying my eyes, but I was filled with the gratitude that I never have to drink again.

I'm so grateful that I'm sober. I never have to drink again. No hangovers, no embarrassment, no lying about my drinking, no hiding bottles, no constant planning. My brain, body, and soul can be truly free and live life to the fullest. I'm out of that cage and I never want to see it again. My relationship with alcohol has morphed from absolute obsession to total disinterest, and, yes, it has been very emotional. Thank you all for not judging my tears.

21 **STOP DIGGING**

I often think about why I drank for so long before I finally stopped. The simple answer is that for many years I could drink as much as I wanted and still maintain a comfortable life that was acceptable to me.

We all need to hit our bottom before we turn around and climb out of the hole we've dug for ourselves. Denial and addiction are extremely cunning at keeping us down and want nothing more than to have us alone, in the dark, feeling hopeless so that we keep drinking and it can suck us dry. Our addicted brain can come up with dozens of reasons and rationalizations as to why we should keep using and worry about quitting some other day. That's the nature of addiction — coupled with an extreme social stigma judging those who are suffering, and we seem to have an army of obstacles to overcome to get started on recovering.

I'm here to say that it's just not that hard to get started. Stop overthinking it and just do it. The key is to do it with others. Fighting this compulsion by yourself is not likely going to work. I tried to for years and every person that

I've ever met in recovery attributes some sort of fellowship (AA is a prime example) as key to their progress. It takes a village and you can absolutely quit with the support and help of others who are on the same road, seeking the same goals.

I'll leave you with a short bit that I wrote about my son. He took a long time to realize he needed to get help. I would sometimes sit alone on a cold night and wonder about where he might be or if he was well. During those times, it helped me to write. Below is something I wrote about what he might have been thinking on those nights when I was thinking about how much I love him.

--

I'm cold, in the rain, and wondering how I got here. I'd give anything to instantly be like I was so long ago — safe, warm, and home with my family. A shadow clouds my brain and tells me that I'm not that person anymore, and the journey is too far and complicated — come back to me and forget about it all. It will be easier for everyone. I do. It isn't.

--

Start today by putting down the shovel — just stop digging and turn around. The body is the most amazing machine ever and it will recover far more quickly than you can imagine. You are never too far gone. We can heal and become far stronger than we ever thought possible. We deserve an amazing life. Do it for yourself and for those that need and love you.

22 WHAT KIND OF ALCOHOLIC ARE YOU?

Hi, my name is Tom, and I'm a high functioning alcoholic (HFA).

I've recently come to take issue with the need to label and categorize our type of alcoholism. Am I a problem drinker (not an alcoholic), a high functioning alcoholic (a secret alcoholic whose life appears to be well in order), or a straight up vanilla alcoholic (true alcoholic who loses complete control and drinks until they black out)? Am I alcoholic-ish?

Aside from wanting to categorize, I don't think it makes much of a difference. The bottom line is that if you want to stop drinking, but cannot stop and stay stopped, then you are an alcoholic. Why complicate it? If you can't stop, then you will eventually progress your drinking until you hit bottom and can no longer deny that you have a problem. Highly functioning alcoholics are like train wrecks in slow motion. It takes longer, but they end up at the same place having become much less functional. A five-year journey may take them decades, but they get there.

We should stop using the term 'true alcoholic'. It's hurting people. Alcoholics have enough issues with denial to split hairs like this. It's like saying, "I smoke crack three times per day and I cannot stop, but I haven't lost everything important to me in my life, so I don't have an addiction problem." An attitude like that will most certainly lead to an extremely obvious addiction problem. These artificial categories make those who have issues with belonging and denial stray from the herd when they need the most help. Let's stop comparing drinkalog stories and focus on the goal of helping each other.

Everyone has a different bottom. Some lose everything — their house, car, spouse, family, health, freedom — you name it. Others simply become sick and tired of the physical and mental toll that being a secret alcoholic takes on you — secretly drinking, hiding the evidence, making excuses for your hangovers, dropping the ball at work, thinking about alcohol constantly as you plan your daily life around getting drunk. Either way is a complete grind and waste of a life.

Anyone with the courage to face their issues with alcohol, no matter who they are, deserves the complete support of other alcoholics in order to get sober. Please don't ever question if someone is a true alcoholic or not. It's a destructive question, and you might be helping that person pick up a drink.

23 YMBAAI - YOU MIGHT BE AN ALCOHOLIC IF

Humor is an essential part of life and I've also found it to be a fantastic tool in my recovery from drinking.

In recovery groups, people frequently tell the story of when their alcohol use caused them to hit bottom, which is the lowest possible point in their lives. Each bottom is different and these stories can be heartbreakingly sad. They illustrate how bad their experience truly was and often tend to mix in comic relief to prevent both the teller and the listener from becoming overly uncomfortable. People often laugh at the details that they recognize as past addict behavior which are meant to be humorous.

I'm no psychologist, but I feel the reason for the humor is that it brings us closer together. Sharing these personal tragic details can be quite emotional and requires getting out of our comfort zone. So, while we laugh, it is a supportive laugh because we have deep compassion for this person's journey. Heavy drinkers are frequently excellent bullshitters and often take things to the extreme.

It's just how we are wired. We have spent many hours drinking and jawing with others telling engaging stories that most often contain some amount of exaggeration and humor. We totally get humor.

One of my favorite resources in my recovery is the podcast *Recovery Elevator* (see the Resources chapter for more details). It is truly must listen material for anyone wishing to stop drinking. One of my favorite things about Paul's podcast is what he calls "You might be an alcoholic if" where his guests, at the end of their interview, make up a joke where they complete the sentence "You might be an alcoholic if _____". For example, "You might be an alcoholic if you lie to your doctor about your drinking". The reason these jokes are so funny is because most any heavy drinker will recognize the behavior and think, "Yeah, I could totally see that happening!"

Here are some of my own custom YMBAAI lines based on my past drinking experience and the occasional news headline that made me think — hmmm, that person must have been hammered. Enjoy!

You might be an alcoholic if you find yourself drinking wine from a Pringles can at 6:30am while riding an electric scooter in a Walmart's parking lot.

You might be an alcoholic if you think that you are NOT an alcoholic because you don't drink during the day.

You might be an alcoholic if you go around telling other alcoholics, "I am not an alcoholic."

You might be an alcoholic if you haven't stopped drinking since Clinton was in office.

You might be an alcoholic if you have ever told someone that you love them more than drinking.

You might be an alcoholic if it takes multiple trips to move your weekly recycling to the curb for pick up.

You might be an alcoholic if you always know precisely how long it's been since your last drink.

You might be an alcoholic if you conveniently hide booze in your closet.

You might be an alcoholic if your doctor tells you that drinking has caused you to lose the feeling in three of your fingers, and your first thought is that you still have seven left.

You might be an alcoholic if your holiday plans include kegs and cases of wine.

You might be an alcoholic if your restaurant food bill pales in comparison to your bar tab.

You might be an alcoholic if you get so drunk on the family church camping trip that you end up packing up the family and sneaking away early the next morning in order to avoid further embarrassment.

You might be an alcoholic if you decide where to go out for dinner based on the double martini specials.

You might be an alcoholic if your favorite local martini bar, out of nowhere, institutes a new three-drink maximum policy. I'm not kidding. They even printed t-shirts.

You might be an alcoholic if you call in sick every other Monday due to some random set of illnesses that are only linked by the fact that they are brought on by alcohol.

You might be an alcoholic if you dearly love all your relatives but cannot remember the details of your reunion get-togethers.

You might be an alcoholic if you start buying your booze at a different store because you personally know one of the new checkers.

You might be an alcoholic if your first priority when vacationing is to fully stock the bar.

You might be an alcoholic if you have booze automatically shipped to your house.

You might be an alcoholic if you have actually worn out cork screws.

You might be an alcoholic if a case of wine is not enough to get you through your Christmas week off.

You might be an alcoholic if you lie to your doctor about how much you drink.

You might be an alcoholic if your definition of social drinking is that you are not drinking alone.

You might be an alcoholic if you haven't seen (or remembered) the New Year's Eve ball drop in years.

You might be an alcoholic if you ever brush your teeth in an effort to hide the scent of alcohol.

You might be an alcoholic if you put your glass of wine in the microwave in order to prevent fruit flies from getting into it while you drive to pick up your daughter from her evening dance class.

You might be an alcoholic if you no longer remember your dreams upon waking up.

You might be an alcoholic if you haven't seen the sunrise for years.

You might be an alcoholic if you have no answer when someone asks you what you do for fun.

You might be an alcoholic if all the waiters in your town already know your drink order without your having to ask.

You might be an alcoholic if you can't recall which TV series episodes that you have already binged or plan to binge even as you are possibly rewatching them.

You might be an alcoholic if people tell you that you do NOT have a drinking problem.

You might be an alcoholic if you keep bottle openers and cork screws in your suitcase toiletry bag.

You might be an alcoholic if you have upgraded to first class because of the expedited drink service.

You might be an alcoholic if a full open bar has you salivating like a world class 'all you can eat' buffet.

You might be an alcoholic if you store spare bottles in your car trunk during the cooler months.

You might be an alcoholic if you disguise booze in order to sneak it into parks and sporting events.

You might be an alcoholic if decorating the Christmas tree involves bottles of wine.

You might be an alcoholic if the ghost of Bacchus anxiously awakens you almost every night at 3:30am.

You might be an alcoholic if your friends invite you to a weekend long 'drink and shoot'.

You might be an alcoholic if the idea of binge watching all five seasons of *Breaking Bad* in a single weekend seems like a completely normal thing to do.

You might be an alcoholic if you think there's 'no point' in just one drink.

You might be an alcoholic if, while driving home drunk from your company Christmas party, you stop to grab a Big Mac, which unfortunately arrives with onions on it, so you call the police, get in a fist fight with them when they arrive, and spend the night in jail. The next morning you have no memory of the incident and state you are not a violent person.

24 MUSIC CAN SET YOU FREE

Music has played a huge part in my recovery. I primarily rely on it for two reasons — both to feel good and to remember. It gets me motivated but also has allowed me to get through some tough times.

I read somewhere that I could best get past negative emotions by feeling them. In other words, rather than ignoring them and pushing them down, doing the opposite. You fully feel and engage with those feelings, and by doing that, they lose their power over you. So, in other words, don't sugar-coat and push your feelings aside. In the past, alcohol helped me to numb my feelings. I have learned that it's better to ride them out and you will soon set yourself free.

I have put together a few of my favorite recovery songs below. These songs motivate me, remind me of where I was, where I am, and where I want to go. Some are sad, some mention booze directly, and some are just be-bop happy. I recommend you listen to each song as you read my take on it. Make you own playlists and see if music works for you. It sure has for me. I listen to it all the time.

Below is a list of songs and why they are on my playlist.

"Leave a Light On" - Tom Walker
https://www.youtube.com/watch?v=nqnkBdExjws

This is a very sad and powerful song. Bottoms are often heart breaking due to their extreme nature. The obsessed drinker often suffers terribly before deciding to save themselves. This song reminds me of the destructive power of drugs and alcohol and to help those around me. We are never too far gone to save ourselves, and there is help for us when we decide that we need it. The light is always on.

"Maybe It's Time" - Bradley Cooper
https://www.youtube.com/watch?v=RdljoTFMhO4

When I first heard this song, I took up learning how to play the guitar. My goal, God help me, is to play and sing this song to my AA home group. I am reminded of the 'maybe' time in my life when I knew that there was a problem with my drinking, but I had not yet committed to changing. In reality, maybe usually means 'not yet'.

"Trouble Me" - 10,000 Maniacs (MTV Unplugged Version)
https://www.youtube.com/watch?v=DPcK0sU3jEw

So much of my recovery has been a head game with myself. I've always thought of myself as a strong independent survivor who doesn't need to rely on anyone else. No doubt that's why it took me decades to decide to quit.

I found my first higher power within ten minutes of my first AA meeting. A month later, I discovered another in nature and meditation. I found my third when I nearly died in the ER. This song reminds me to give away things I can't handle to my HP and to daily feel that power to sooth my mind and soul. I imagine my HP sending me this message to trouble him with things that I cannot control.

"Closer To You" - The Wallflowers
https://www.youtube.com/watch?v=lhouUpAdg9E

Ok, this is most likely a love song and not about recovery at all, but the thing about recovery is that EVERYTHING in your life is about recovery!

This song speaks to me. It's my voice right now speaking to the more recovered version of myself that I am intended to be. I continue to recover and I get closer and closer to that person every day.

"I Will Survive" - Cake
https://www.youtube.com/watch?v=7KJjVMqNIgA

Overall, Cake is my favorite band — maybe it's the liberal use of horns and cowbells! I turn this one on when I need to dig deep and give alcohol some shit in order to get by. I feel that you need to approach sobriety like you approach survival, no half measures, or you are just continuing to run on the hamster wheel of addiction. FU alcohol, I will survive!

Gloria Gaynor's version also rocks!

"Man That I've Become" - Nick Lowe
https://www.youtube.com/watch?v=_QlzfsFZrQw

Near the end of my drinking, I turned into something that I would not like to ever become again. It happens so glacially, one day and one drink at a time and before you know it you wake up and suddenly realize that you have truly fucked yourself. You no longer want to be the man that you've become.

"Brother" - NeedToBreathe
https://www.youtube.com/watch?v=61Wm_qlVD4Q

You can't fight this alone and we all need help and to help others to make this journey. We are all truly brothers and sisters in this fight to restore ourselves to having full, healthy, and productive lives. We give each other hope and strength.

"Last Drink" - Bastard Bearded Irishmen
https://www.youtube.com/watch?v=x6O96ACQY8M

Alcohol is all fun and games until the end comes. Every alcoholic has struggled with the goal of the last drink. For many of us, the last drink chooses the time, not us. Yeah, he died of alcoholism — don't do that!

"Survivor" - Destiny's Child
https://www.youtube.com/watch?v=Wmc8bQoL-J0

Another FU tribute aimed directly at alcohol. At some point you may hit a low when you have tried all your coping mechanisms and reached out to those who can help you, and you still can't shake a chronic case of the fuck-its. At this point, you will need to decide if you are a survivor or not. Perhaps this song could be the tipping point that helps to keep you sober.

"Otherside" - Post Malone
https://www.youtube.com/watch?v=9Kid43pzGjk

"We're no strangers to the flame, we will never be the same, If we make it through"

That pretty much sums up recovery. Led to it by pain, you must fight your way through to the glorious fields on the other side. The journey will completely change who you are and how you think by the time you get there.

"It Aint the Whiskey" - Gary Allan
https://www.youtube.com/watch?v=m3Xr67jp1Fo

Yeah, I have eclectic music tastes. Good messages are where you find them.

This song would make any AA fellowship member smile as we all know it aint the whiskey. It reminds me that the reason I drank had little to do with alcohol itself which was simply the tool that I chose to not deal with reality. It takes us a long time to truly understand that it's not the substances. It's us. That is often the last place that we look for the answer.

"It Don't Matter" - Southern Discomfort
https://www.youtube.com/watch?v=WOPN24hyspU

Don't hold on to pain, but let it go into the air! Feel and process it and then let it go. That shit will kill you otherwise (for sure).

"Don't Leave Home" - Dido
https://www.youtube.com/watch?v=tLpsDamWdIM

This sweet sounding song truly captures the essence of alcohol and drugs from my perspective. It speaks to you in a sweet comforting voice and promises to take care of all your problems and keep you safe, warm, and happy. Stay home with me it says, you don't need anyone else.

It all works so well, until it doesn't. Alcohol wants you alone and all to itself until it sucks you dry.

"ANXIETY" - blackbear
https://www.youtube.com/watch?v=XKQa1vx-oNY

"I can't eat, I can't sleep, you give me anxiety." I would wake up at 3:30am convinced that I was having a heart attack. Drenched in sweat and feeling like my heart, lungs, and brain were about to explode. Alcohol causes INTENSE anxiety once you are addicted to it. It's a special nightly Catherine's Wheel of Hell. Anxiety causes you to drink, which gives a short reprieve, followed by even more intense anxiety, rinse and repeat until it eventually kills you. I don't ever want to forget about that or feel that way again.

"Downtown" - Macklemore
https://www.youtube.com/watch?v=JGhoLcsr8GA

Cut loose and have fun. That's what life is all about after all! I had a moped for a time, and there is nothing so ridiculous and fun at exactly the same time.

Living and partying is going downtown sober, making new memories with friends and loved ones, having fun, and remembering it all!

25 **AT ONE YEAR**

One year is a big milestone. At that point we have a greater than 50 percent chance of remaining sober for the rest of our lives. I'll take those odds because I had a near 100 percent chance of getting drunk every day for over a decade. I have lived and changed more in this first year of not drinking than in the previous decade. If I had not lived through it myself, I would hardly believe it. I'd like to give some insight into what I see as my personal phases of recovery.

At first, I just wanted to stop. I didn't care why I drank, but I came to understand that my life had become shit. I understood that I could not continue as a heavy drinker. Alcohol was such a key part of my identity that I was truly lost without it. At the end of my drinking, I no longer participated in hobbies, meaningful socialization, volunteer work, or much of anything fun. I took vacations to some of the most beautiful places on Earth, and all that I cared about was more drinking. I was devoted to nothing but drinking whenever I could. One morning after a weekend of hard drinking, I had a moment of clarity where I came to fully believe and understand that I no longer wanted to live that way. I was fifty years old and had wasted enough of my life and potential by checking out of my life on a daily basis. I could no longer accept the reality of what my life had become and I wanted change. I had hit my bottom.

Then, I stopped. That first week was rough for me. Although most heavy drinkers are able to quit without requiring medical assistance, it is a good idea to see your doctor before quitting. In my case, I knew no better, and decided to quit cold turkey. I laid in bed for three days with what were likely withdrawal symptoms, but at the time I thought was a bad virus. Headache, nausea, exhaustion, and a lot of sweating were my primary symptoms. After five days, however, I felt better than I had in many years. In short order, I looked better, I felt better, food tasted better, and sleep became better. I could hardly believe it. I felt ten years younger. I began to feel better physically than I had in a long time.

After I stopped drinking and started to work on my recovery, I became dedicated and completely devoted to it. Recovery was my new focus in life, and staying sober was my highest priority. I started writing about my experiences, went to AA meetings, and met new people in person and online. I replaced my addiction to alcohol with a healthy addiction to recovering from alcohol. I used my natural tendency to focus intensely and dedicate myself obsessively to focus on and jump start my recovery. My mind and my physical body started to feel great now that they were longer under daily attack from toxins, and life just got better.

Early on, I often had incredibly realistic dreams about drinking, and I would wake up in an absolute panic quite certain that I had drank. I learned how to deal with cravings. After drinking so much for so long, I needed to work on new ways to cope with the stress and strain of daily life without relying on alcohol. I replaced alcohol with LaCroix, reengaged with old hobbies and friends, went on long hikes, and took long walks at the lake. I made sure that I kept myself busy with all the extra time I now had from having cleared my daily drinking calendar. I took it one day at a time.

In the beginning, I thought daily about not drinking in the same way that I had previously thought about drinking. After a few weeks, it started to get easier. I began to regularly attend AA meetings. It helped so much to know that I was not alone and that I could reach out for help whenever I needed it. I was feeling my way into this new world of sobriety. To be honest, AA can seem a bit like a cult at first. Meetings have their own sayings and phrases that can catch you off guard until you become familiar with them. I made friends at meetings who encouraged me to get a sponsor to which I replied, "This spiritual stuff is great and all, but I just need you to show me how to stop drinking!" I was looking for a quick fix and didn't yet see the value in having a sponsor or working the steps.

After the first month, I started to feel so much better physically. I felt rested because I was soundly sleeping throughout the night — a solid eight hours of continuous uninterrupted sleep! This is a luxury no alcoholic gets due to the constant effort required in attempting to manage anxiety. The same alcohol that you drink for relaxation before bed results in your waking up in the middle of the night feeling like you are having a heart attack. I can't really state strongly enough how MUCH more rested I felt after having slept so poorly for so long. I spent many years getting drunk each night — staying up until 1am drinking, falling asleep or passing out, restlessly tossing and turning, waking up every few hours, and then greeting the day already exhausted before it even began. Being an alcoholic was like running a marathon every week — so draining all day all the time. I have no idea how I managed to maintain my job and other life responsibilities during those last few years of drinking.

It was also at this time that I started dreaming again! When I was drinking, I had stopped dreaming. No dreams of flying, or falling in love, or swimming in a pink ocean with silver sparkling dolphins! I only had occasional nightmares where I woke up drenched in sweat with my body heaving from a pounding chest and rapid breathing brought on by intense anxiety. I slept A LOT in the beginning of my sobriety. I was making up for a decade of lost quality sleep. I still vividly recall the first time that my body woke up naturally, fully rested one Saturday morning; it was absolute bliss and total contentment. One of my friends in recovery jokes that sleep is the only drug that we have left. There is nothing to me as refreshing or empowering as to be well rested. Sleep is perhaps the only healthy way to temporarily check out of your life, travel to another world, and safely return in better condition than when you left.

With all that rest, better nutrition, and having shaved at least 1,000 calories per day from my diet, I was not only feeling better, I was also looking better. Better skin, better color, better attitude, lost weight, it was all good. I had much better mental focus and productivity at work. My hair and fingernails started to grow again and my eyes sparkled. I woke up early and went to bed early. It was a magical time of healing and recovery. It was also during this time that I started to work with a sponsor and to help others in recovery. Having the right sponsor and working the steps is like having access to the world's best therapist, all for free. I had tried expensive therapy in the past in an effort to stop my drinking, but it never came close to working. It's impossible for someone who has not walked this path to know what it is like. The steps for me were the key to getting through to the other side from addiction to sobriety, and I needed a guide who had walked that path themselves.

At five months, I hit a rocky patch. My emotions went in to high gear. I was all over the place, crying one minute, laughing the next. Some days I felt unable to control my emotions much at all. This was alarming for me as few who know me would describe me as overly emotional. I now know that part of this could have been post-acute withdrawal symptoms (PAWS) which is common for alcoholics that drank for many years. I also no longer had my old friend alcohol to numb the problems that I wanted to ignore, so I had to fully feel them instead. Lastly, my brain was in WTF mode trying to adjust to its new chemical environment. I needed to develop new coping mechanisms. When I was using alcohol to indirectly control my dopamine levels, my brain stopped taking on that responsibility. The brain now needed to re-engage as my body readjusted to its new chemical situation. There were so many changes — chemical, physical, and mental. It's a bit like changing out the engine while at the same time flying the airplane! There are going to be some rough patches as we figure out why we drank and develop new coping mechanisms for those reasons. I had good days and bad days, but my worst day sober was far better than any day when I was a heavy drinker.

A key mental trick for me was to play the tape forward. In my darkest moments when I really felt like I needed a drink, I thought about how that would go. First one, then another and another, and then who knows. Once the monster has escaped its cage, most anything could happen. I had no idea how long it would take to stop again although I did know that the next effort would be even more difficult than the last. No, it was much better for me to push through those emotions and process them through anger, rage, crying, exercise, meditation, or whatever it took because each time that I did face these feelings, they became easier to deal with the next time they appeared. I could see everything continually getting better with time and effort.

At six months, I hit a plateau. It was a magical time. I was stable, working my recovery, learning new coping mechanisms, making new sober friends, and reconnecting with old friends that I had pushed out of my life years ago. I was getting my shit together! It was a new me and it was amazing. I rekindled old hobbies and started new ones, such as hiking and regular exercise. I lost considerable weight and looked and felt better than I had in fifteen years. My brain was on fire with clarity and focus. I became much stronger physically. I started hiking trails that I had not been able to do comfortably in many years. My neighbors, coworkers, and family started noticing the changes in me, both mentally and physically. I was so much more present for my wife and children, and they often thanked me for being there for them. It was the little things really — helping with homework, spending time chatting in the evenings, walking the dog together, taking early morning trips, so many things that my drinking had prevented in the past. I continued to connect with others in recovery and no longer felt cravings at all. I had no desire to drink. I now looked at drinking, at least the way that I had done it, as a sad pathetic way to have lived, and I felt shame that I had done so for so long.

By this time in my sobriety, I had dealt with just about any situation related to alcohol that I was likely to encounter. All my acquaintances knew that I no longer drank. I told family and friends I had given up alcohol. I didn't tell most that I was an alcoholic, only that I no longer drank because I didn't like how alcohol made me feel. I could go a bar with colleagues and comfortably order a seltzer with cranberry while they drank alcohol with no jealousy or concern of missing out. I spent a week alone in Las Vegas for a huge conference. It was the most fun that I'd ever had there. I stayed up late, saw the sites, went to concerts and clubs, gambled, toured the town, and yet I was easily able to get up at 6am the next morning. I met so many fun, sober people on that trip. We gambled, chatted, had dinner, and really connected in a way that never happens when you are drinking heavily. I never announced to any of them that I was a recovering alcoholic. I just didn't drink, and it never came up.

Once I was fully living life and no longer constantly looking for my next drink, I found that I effortlessly met many others who were doing the same thing. When I was a drunk, I tended to be drawn to and attract other drunks. I still had tough days here and there, but I had developed coping mechanisms that allowed me to be less and less affected by them. I discovered that if I was feeling down and in a funk that helping others made me instantly feel much better. Whether it was giving someone a pep talk on the bus, delivering food to a shelter, or reaching out to someone at a meeting, it greatly improved my outlook. You definitely get much more than you give when you help someone.

At nine months I gained deeper insights about my drinking. I saw many of my past behaviors and ways of thinking with a new clarity. For the first time, I began to better understand at a much deeper level why I drank so much for so long. It was much like peeling on onion. The more I recovered, the more I learned and understood about myself, the better I saw why I drank in the first place. Getting sober is very much a spiritual journey as you accept yourself, forgive yourself, and grow your understanding of yourself and your relationships both past and present. I resolved resentments by processing them and letting them go. Looking at situations where I had been wounded and where I intentionally hurt others allowed me to see past those individual issues to more underlying core issues. Many slights that we have felt or put upon others have a common cause and I started to see those causes.

I came to understand that both the problem and the solution were standing right in front of me — in the mirror. It wasn't my fault, but somehow as a child I had swallowed more pain than I could handle. Being teased and feeling like an outsider had caused a pain in me that wouldn't heal. Those experiences took over much of my world as a kid, and I never wanted to feel that way again. I got stuck on feeling unworthy, less than, and not accepted. To deal with these feelings, I became an actor and a people pleaser — becoming what I thought people wanted me to be in order to ensure that they would accept me. I decided my own feelings didn't matter. The only thing that mattered was being accepted. Over time, I developed these and other flawed coping mechanisms, including my new friend alcohol, which worked spectacularly well to solve my problems. Alcohol filled me with confidence because I felt like I belonged and was accepted.

Like so many alcoholics, I hated parts of myself. From the outside, no one would have known. I hid my feelings and fears from everyone. I was my own worst enemy for most of my life. I had internalized this negative thinking about myself as a child and those thinking patterns led me to worship alcohol because it provided relief. I had hidden my true self in plain sight for so long that I no longer truly remembered who I really was. Gaining this understanding provided a measure of closure for me, but also a deep sadness and empathy for the child-like part of me that is buried down deep in my soul. I can deal with my irrational thinking today, but part of me will always have a negative emotional response about not fitting in. It's like having experienced an intense electrical shock from a badly wired light fixture. Even after it has been repaired, I am still leery of flipping that particular switch. I intellectually understand I am not the boy of my youth, but my subconscious still remembers the emotional pain.

At one year, I felt a great sense of pride at what I had accomplished. I also felt a huge debt of gratitude for those that helped me accomplish it and relief that I had saved myself and would never have to drink again. I got my one-year chip and birthday cake at my local AA meeting! I was no longer worried about myself around alcohol or drinking. I had grown enough that I knew I would not drink as long as I kept living honestly with myself. If I started to once again lie to others about who I was, that would make it all too easy to lie to myself and start drinking again. That is the one fear that all alcoholics, in my opinion, need to share if they are going to stay sober. We must maintain great respect for the power of alcohol to destroy all that we have recovered. We cannot fall into the 'just one' trap because there is no such thing as just one for us. It's like the fable of the scorpion and the frog. Alcohol's true nature, particularly for us, is a destroyer and it cannot possibly be anything else.

When you get sober, you have a lot of free time on your hands and that provides an excellent opportunity for essential personal growth. We need to spiritually grow our way permanently out of this drinking problem. I could not revert back to the person that I was before I drank because that person had some serious self-worth problems and would quite likely be headed down the same path to alcohol once again. I knew I needed to change. When I was drinking, I wasn't really me. I was living as a checked-out version of a person avoiding pain. Accepting this and working to figure out who I am today and what I want for my life has been extremely empowering. Discovering my true self and living authentically brings great peace and confidence. Figuring out what I truly like, what I truly do not like, and creating boundaries for myself and others has been such an eye-opening experience.

Treating everything you had previously accepted as fact with much critical thinking opens new possibilities. It was a big change for me. In the past, my first thought was assuming I needed to protect myself by fitting in or ensuring that I was valued and admired by all those around me. I was not true to myself and my nature. It took me some time to figure this out, but I believe we need to choose and direct what we are becoming as we grow and recover. I must be open and vulnerable, connect with others on the same journey, believe in myself, and believe in them and where we are going. I must move forward and refuse to waste time in my life with toxic thinking or toxic people. I know where that path leads. I've taken it already. The longer I continue to connect, live life, and turn off negative thinking, the easier everything becomes. Everyone has their own path and struggles, and no one can tell you how easy or difficult yours will be. It is for you to discover and become who you are truly meant to be. Our natural state as humans is to be spiritual, connected, loving, and loved. We all deserve to be happy, and we have the power to fix ourselves and bring about that change. All it takes is desire and effort. Anyone can do this for themselves.

Will I remain sober a year from now or five or ten years from now? I think so, but I don't intend to ever take my sobriety for granted. The best way to prevent a relapse is to live my best life now in the moment, and the future will take care of itself. I know the spiritual program I have been working this last year has taken me many miles on my journey already. I am so far away from where I was one year ago when I began. I will continue to work my recovery because I truly love what it has done for my life already. I cannot imagine what I will discover to free my thinking even further in the years to come. As far as alcohol goes, it sounds overly simplistic, but if I never again drink alcohol, I will never again have a problem with it. I never planned on becoming an alcoholic — no one does. It just slowly happens over time one sip at a time. No amount of alcohol is safe for someone looking to numb their pain. The important thing for me to remember is this: Today I no longer have a drinking problem, but I can find one very quickly. It all starts with a single sip.

26 **RESOURCES**

There are so many amazing resources available related to alcohol and recovery. Here are a few of my favorites. This is not an exhaustive list but it will get you well on your way to better understanding alcohol and your relationship with it.

If you do only one thing today, start listening to the *Recovery Elevator* podcast. There is no need to go in order, just jump in on any topic that interests you. Paul interviewed me on episode #207 of his *Recovery Elevator* podcast — check it out if you would like to hear my story in my own voice. If you are up for doing two things today, go to an AA meeting as well! :)

"Recovery Elevator" Podcast by Paul Churchill

There are many podcasts related to recovery, but this is my favorite. Paul Churchill is himself a recovering alcoholic and he brings a passion and mission to recovery that is truly inspiring. There are over two hundred episodes that cover all recovery topics and feature interviews with those who have been in recovery from days (or hours) to years. This is an excellent and perhaps THE resource to begin to deprogram your mind into no longer desiring alcohol. Paul's insights and guests reveal alcohol's true nature.

Paul also runs an amazing online recovery community called Cafe:RE. I am a member and have found it an extremely valuable tool. I can get as much contact and support as I need with others in recovery by simply pulling out my phone. Cafe:RE also regularly organizes in-person meetups and regular weekly webinars to connect, discuss topics, and get to know each other better. It's worth checking out to see if it works for you.

You can find all the podcasts here: https://www.recoveryelevator.com/podcasts/

"This Naked Mind" By Annie Grace

Annie's explanation of the conscious and unconscious mind and how they relate to drinking was key to my understanding of how I stopped drinking.

She also has an excellent podcast by the same name where she interviews guests about their experiences with alcohol and she offers online programs and courses.

You can find her book here: https://www.amazon.com/This-Naked-Mind-Discover-Happiness-ebook/dp/B077VTJC8P

Alcoholics Anonymous

You can't do it alone. It is so much easier when you

connect with others. If it weren't for AA, I would still be drinking.

If you are concerned about your drinking and have no idea what to do about it, do yourself a favor and go to meeting in order to see what it's all about.

Find the right meeting and start your recovery TODAY! https://www.aa.org/

"Alcohol Explained" by William Porter

This is my overall favorite book on alcohol. Easy to read, no-nonsense scientific analysis of how it all works and how to beat it. https://www.amazon.com/Alcohol-Explained-William-Porter/dp/1516997190

"Addiction Unlimited" podcast by Angela Pugh

Angela has an amazing conversational style of delivery and her podcast is chock full of incredible information on all topics related to addiction and getting sober. She is also a recovering alcoholic who offers her podcast, interventions, and sobriety coaching. She even runs her own sober living houses!

Check out her site, she is quite an amazing person and I am so grateful for her dedication and insights. http://addictionunlimited.com/episodes/

ABOUT THE AUTHOR

Bill Williams is a longtime professional software developer that lives in the Pacific Northwest. If you watch videos online, you have probably used his software. This is his first book which he wrote to help others who are tired of struggling with alcohol. If you liked the book, please take a minute to rate and review it on Amazon. Your rating will help others to find it, read these essays, and start their journey to become sober.

Printed in Great Britain
by Amazon